Thomas Leach

A Short Sketch of the Tractarian Upheaval

Thomas Leach

A Short Sketch of the Tractarian Upheaval

ISBN/EAN: 9783743305571

Manufactured in Europe, USA, Canada, Australia, Japa

Cover: Foto ©ninafisch / pixelio.de

Manufactured and distributed by brebook publishing software (www.brebook.com)

Thomas Leach

A Short Sketch of the Tractarian Upheaval

SHORT SKETCH

OF

THE TRACTARIAN UPHEAVAL.

A SHORT SKETCH

OF THE

RACTARIAN UPHEAVAL

BY

THOMAS LEACH, B.A.

Late Scholar of Corpus Christi College, Cambridge, Vicar of Burton-in-Lonsdale.

London:
BEMROSE AND SONS, 23, OLD BAILEY;
AND AT DERBY.

—

1887.

(All Rights Reserved.)

LONDON
BEMROSE AND SONS,
23, OLD BAILEY; AND AT DERBY.

PREFACE.

It has seemed to the author that a short work, such as the one attempted in these pages, might possibly be found useful by such persons who have heard of the *Oxford Movement*, of *The Tracts for the Times*, and of the secession of Dr. Newman to Rome, but who possess little definite or systematic knowledge of these matters.

Much undoubtedly has been written upon the personages, and the events of that great era, but the information lies scattered in the pages of many different books, some of these only to be obtained at rare intervals from the second-hand dealers.

The author does not profess allegiance to any one party in the church, nor is he conscious of any preference for one above another.

It has been his endeavour in this short sketch, simply to record facts, and the impressions created by those facts on the minds of the ablest men of all schools of thought. He has found himself unable to invent any theory, or discover any general law, which would cover and account for all the features of the Movement; and has, therefore, been spared the temptation to twist facts into accordance with any such preconceived explanation.

It is almost needless to say that he does not profess complete agreement with all the sentiments which he has quoted from so many different writers.

BURTON-IN-LONSDALE,
   Dec., 1887.

TABLE OF CONTENTS.

Chapter I.—THE "WHEN."

Chapter II.—THE "WHERE."

Chapter III.—THE "BY WHOM."

Chapter IV.—THE "HOW."

Chapter V.—THE PROGRESS OF THE UNDULATION.

Chapter VI.—THE RESULTS.

LIST OF WORKS FROM WHICH EXTRACTS ARE TAKEN IN THE FOLLOWING PAGES.

"THE TRACTS FOR THE TIMES"
APOLOGIA PRO VITA SUA . . . . *J. H. Newman*
REMAINS OF RICHARD HURRELL FROUDE .
       Ed. *J. H. Newman & J. Keble*
MEMOIR OF REV. JOHN KEBLE . . . *Sir J. T. Coleridge*
REMINISCENCES, CHIEFLY OF ORIEL COLLEGE . *T. Mozley*
THE NEMESIS OF FAITH . . . . . *J. A. Froude*
THE OXFORD COUNTER-REFORMATION . . *J. A. Froude*
ESSAYS IN ECCLESIASTICAL BIOGRAPHY . *Sir J. Stephen*
MEMOIR OF MARK PATTISON . . . . *Pattison*
LIFE OF DEAN HOOK . . . . . . *Stephens*
LIFE OF BISHOP WILBERFORCE . . . . *Ashwell*
LETTERS AND MEMORIES OF CHARLES KINGSLEY *Kingsley*
LIFE OF FREDERICK DENISON MAURICE . . *Maurice*
LIFE OF F. W. ROBERTSON . . . . . *Brooke*
THE CHURCH AND THE WORLD. 1867 . . Ed. *O. Shipley*
A LIFE'S DECISION . . . . . . *Allies*
LIFE OF JAMES FRASER, Bp. OF MANCHESTER *T. Hughes*
MONOGRAPHS . . . . *Lord Houghton*
CELEBRITIES AT HOME. 1st and 2nd Series. . Ed. *Ed. Yates*
A HISTORY OF THE CHURCH OF ENGLAND .
          W. N. Molesworth
THE ENGLISH CHURCH . . . . . *Gresley*
A KEY TO THE POPERY OF OXFORD . . *Peter Maurice*
LIFE OF DANIEL MACMILLAN . . . . *T. Hughes*
PENDENNIS . . . . *Thackeray*
VARIOUS REVIEWS, ARTICLES, AND LETTERS IN
    The Church Quarterly Review, The Guardian,
    Macmillan's Magazine, The Leisure Hour, &c.

THE TRACTARIAN UPHEAVAL.

CHAPTER I.

THE " WHEN."

SPEAKING of the great religious movement, of which during many years he was himself so conspicuously the head and front, and of which in these pages a slight sketch is attempted, Dr. Newman has observed,—" Of course, every event in human affairs has a beginning; and a beginning implies a when, and a where, and a by whom, and a how." The same great teacher has also placed it on record that he has ever considered and kept Sunday, July 14, 1833, as the start of the movement; Mr. Keble having on that day preached the Assize Sermon in the Oxford University Pulpit, which was published under the title of " National Apostacy." We may therefore not unfitly, in this our first chapter, endeavour to valuate the " When " of the movement by a short survey of the times in which it had its birth, and the then condition of matters spiritual and ecclesiastical in England; in the chapters which immediately follow we shall pass by an easy and natural transition to consider the " where," the " by whom," and the " how."

The early part of the present century was essentially an age of practical endeavour rather than of religious excitement, and our great-grandfathers conceived that it was their prime necessity to hold Napoleon at bay, and to preserve at any cost their own liberties and those of other European nationalities, so dangerously threatened by the despot of Corsica; and to a generation engaged in such a struggle ecclesiastical squabbles must have appeared impertinent and idle trifling. In other respects, too, it was one of the most momentous eras of modern history. Greater changes were in progress in the internal economy of Great Britain than had been witnessed in any two preceding centuries, according to an historian, who goes on to describe how—" Agriculture, commerce, manufactures, revenue, and population expanded with an unexampled elasticity. Never before had the material world been made to pay so large a tribute to the material wants of mankind. Under the half-magical power of the steam-engine, works, which would have baffled the muscular strength of all the inhabitants of the globe united, were performed in a narrow district of this narrow island, with an ease, a precision, and a rapidity, emulating some of the mighty operations of nature. Wealth, such as avarice had scarcely pictured in her dreams, was accumulated in those centres of mechanical industry, and the higher class of English society, commercial as well as noble, revelled in a sumptuousness of living, for which a description or an example could be found nowhere but in the fabulous East."

Amid all the triumphant glories, however, of this great epoch of national prosperity and self assertion, the life of the Church by law Established seemed to be withering down towards complete and final extinction. The ground was then occupied by two distinct parties, the Orthodox and the Evangelical, each despising the other, and each strenuously grasping at the government and the preferments of the Church.

The former party, who would now be known as the Historical High Church, or the old High and Dry, were the exponents of the Hanoverian Church and State religion, which made salvation to depend largely on obedience to Acts of Parliament, with but little insistance on the spirituality of the inner life. The High Churchmen of this time were careful in their compliance with the directions of the Book of Common Prayer, but had come to take up a very different position from that which had been occupied by the High Churchmen of the seventeenth century. As was not untruly remarked by the late Bishop Blomfield, the doctrine of the Apostolical succession had gone out with the Nonjurors, who, led by Sancroft, had set an example of disinterested consistency in the reign of William and Mary; and the English Church of the Georgian era had tacitly renounced that doctrine, or did not, at any rate, employ it much in controversy with nonconformists of all denominations. The Orthodox party now urged the claim of the Church to attention and consideration, not so much on the ground of her connection by an unbroken episcopal chain with the Church of the Apostles, as on the fact of her being *by law established*. Frequent struggles with foreign foes are apt to create vigorous national feeling, and to keep alive the remembrance of the fact that nationalities as well as churches owe their existence to God, and are possibly as important in His sight. The state must of necessity be anterior to the Church, and must be reckoned with in any theory of corporate church life; and the fact that any given system of religious worship is approved and enjoined by the powers that be, which are ordained of God, carries a weight to sober common-sense minds, which is not always at once apparent in dogmatic statements about the sanctity and the certainty of an unbroken apostolic succession.

The evangelical party, on the other hand, accepted the Bible and the Prayer Book as the rule of life, but were apt to ignore all interpretation of them save by their own private judgment. They saw the value, and claimed for themselves the advantages, of an ecclesiastical position, though many of them were in point of fact simply ordained dissenters; and though they undoubtedly possessed a certain degree of spiritual life, yet making, as they did, a subjective faith the sole criterion of religion, their acceptance of the doctrines of sacramental grace was little more than nominal. Experiences were at a premium, works at a discount. Those who held the highest and most influential positions in the Church were doing little to strengthen her bulwarks, or to heal her wounds. Archbishops succeeded each other duly in the seat of St. Augustine, but living though they did within a stone's throw of the lowest degradation and the most abject misery of London, they yet found it in their hearts to amass immense fortunes for their children, while they gorged their other relatives with the loaves and fishes placed at their disposal, leaving the Church meanwhile to drift helpless over a sea of ruin.

Gross scandals of every kind abounded: according to Mr. Molesworth the bishoprics and other high dignities of the Church were sold by Mrs. Clark, the mistress of the Duke of York; and some of the clergy had earned their preferments, so it was rumoured, by marriages with ladies who had stood in questionable relationships to the patrons or other influential laymen.

The condition of ecclesiastical fabrics was such as might have been expected. "Let any one call back his mind to the thousand mutilations of the old churches of our fathers, and the desolations which met them at every turn; the galleries; the multiform boxes of the gentry and tradesmen; the drawing-room pew of the squire of the parish, with his sofa and his stove; the mildewed walls; the rotten timbers of the roof, through which the rain made its uninterrupted way. Even cathedrals, *e.g.*, Lichfield, were filled with common church boxes, and women sat promiscuously with the lay clerks and the clergy in seats which accommodated both, without respect of persons. The fonts were overthrown, the sanctuaries were desecrated. On the altar at St. Paul's Cathedral, London, it was no uncommon thing to see hats and cloaks piled up, on occasion of great meetings, as though it were no more than a common table."

Bishop Fleetwood, in his charge in 1710, had observed —" Unless the good public spirit of building, repairing, and adorning churches prevails a great deal more among us, and be more encouraged, an hundred years will bring to the ground an huge number of our churches." He pleaded almost in vain. Bishop Butler, in his famous charge in 1751, quoted these words, and added—" This excellent prelate made this observation forty years ago; and no one, I believe, will imagine that the good spirit he recommended prevails more at present than it did then."

A writer of our own day commenting upon these episcopal utterances gives us several interesting reminiscences of the condition of the Church in his own early years, in the following words :—" I remember the wooden pinnacles which capped the stone buttresses of Canterbury Cathedral in place of those which fell. In a church which I served in Cornwall the walls were held up by wooden props outside, and the snow fell upon the altar between the East wall and the roof. One day a crash almost as loud as the report of a pistol during the prayers, announced the increasing pressure upon a window over the desk. In an Essex church which I served, a lady who worshipped there, and was touched in the head, used to say she was sure it had been a grocer's shop, for it was all green and white like a Stilton cheese. On the leaden roofs of two churches in the Midlands I walked whilst they trembled under my feet. In a Northamptonshire church there were holes in the stone floor, so that one walked up and down in going towards the East end. If our forefathers had not built more durably than we do, few churches would have been now standing. All honour to those who spared nothing, gave of their best, and did their best for the glory of God. As for the altars, they were inferior tables covered with a scanty bit of green or blue baise, and the fonts were the receptacles of hats. It would have been ludicrous, had it not been sad, to contrast the warning texts on the walls bidding people be reverential with the preparation to make them so, and with the state of mind of the parsons and churchwardens who were satisfied with such houses of God. And what shall I say of the pewter flagon or the black bottle, of the one ragged surplice, of the tumble-down filthy pews, excepting that of the squire which contained fire-place and table in the middle? Of the mouldy office books, of the cracked bells, of the orgies of the ringers in the church tower? Of the Christmas holly sprigs stuck into the tops of the pews, as if they were the carcases of beef or mutton? Of the altar used as a table, with inkhorn and pen?"

Church music, too, had fallen upon evil times, for the writer from whom we have just quoted goes on to record how "When I was young there was not a choral service in the diocese except that of the cathedral, about which the less said the better; and I was present when my then bishop told us in his charge that we were none of us to attempt choral service, and that the service of the cathedral, which, by the way, was on the other side of a broad river without a bridge in the diocese, was meant to gratify and suffice all those who had a musical taste." The quality of the music was as unsatisfactory as the quantity. Another writer on the subject tells us how "There was an abundance of good material at hand; many of the psalm tunes of the sixteenth and seventeenth centuries were music of a high order, and for a time they furnished the staple of congregational singing. But, as years rolled on the vocal propensities of the people, curbed and repressed by arbitrary and unauthorized custom, led them to seek the gratification of strange indulgences. Secular music of all sorts, from time to time, was pressed into the Church's service. The music to Macbeth, commonly attributed to Locke, Giga movements from Corelli, snatches from theatrical and operatic compositions, mutilated portions of oratorio music: these, and a mass of other incongruous and unsuitable materials gradually took the place of the genuine psalm tune. Improper selection led to unworthy performance; and in the majority of cases the music heard in churches, though endured by many because of the purpose for which it was used, and the place in which it was used, became a positive infliction on the musical ear, and an object of ridicule to the careless and the profane."

At the beginning of this century the cathedral composers had adopted an effeminate and inferior style, and so the attempts naturally made in ordinary parish churches to imitate the cathedral music of the day, led to a general levelling down of musical taste and perception throughout the country. Such attempts at imitation were, of course, confined chiefly to town churches, those in the country being abandoned to every possible travesty of sacred harmony. In one the congregation would listen in severe and judicial silence to the parson and clerk duet; in another might be heard the harsh grind of the barrel-organ accompanied by the shrill scream of school children; in another might be found the orchestra of fiddle and clarionet, the serpent and the French horn, the basoon and trombone, which, as one of our prelates observed, "Made the bare walls ache with the screech of their discord."

Nor, if we turn to the observance of Church seasons and services, do things seem to have been better than in regard to the points which we have already considered. The Church Almanack would seem to have been entirely forgotten, or to have been shelved in deference to the usages of Society; and as an instance of this neglect it may suffice to mention that in the cathedral city of Lichfield the principal fair of the year took place on Ash Wednesday, and *Ash Wednesday was put off to the next week.*

Mr. Heygate, whom we have already quoted, writes as follows: " I was staying in Spring Gardens in 1841 and 1842, and I knew of no church where I could communicate on Ascension Day except Christ Church, Albany Street, and walking thither I passed the churches with closed doors. I question whether there was a cathedral in England at that time, which had a weekly celebration, and am confident that there was not a daily celebration anywhere. In Essex, where I first served, there was no daily service in the Hundred, and then for a long time only one. Here (Brighstone), from the time of the Reformation until Bishop Wilberforce became rector in 1830, there were only four or five Communions in the year; no daily service until Bishop Moberly became rector in 1866. He adopted a fortnightly Communion; but there was no weekly Communion and no celebration on Ascension Day until 1870."

In some out-of-the-way country districts which had not been deeply affected by the Wesleyan Revival, the custom, inherited from the Old Faith, of bowing to the altar on entering a church still survived, and the writer remembers its observance by a few aged persons, in a retired rural parish five-and-thirty years ago. In the majority of churches, however, any act of special reverence was the exception which proved the general rule of careless profanity. The Englishman would only too often walk in with a nonchalant air, smell the inside of his hat for a moment or two, fling himself indifferently into the corner of his pew, and then begin smiling and bowing to his acquaintances. The irreverent entrance was but a sample of the conduct throughout. Instead of kneeling to pray, most of the people sat at their ease with the most perfect coolness, or at the best contributed their share in the formation of what is termed "the national custom of bending forward in Church," which was faithfully observed by our own Royal Family in Westminster Abbey on a memorable occasion last June. Those who desired to do right showed, by the ludicrous mistakes which they made, their ignorance of the proprieties, or even the meaning of the service. Some of them would sit when they ought to have stood, or would stand when they should have sat; some would repeat the exhortation or absolution after the minister—thus exhorting and absolving themselves.

Then as to doctrine. To quote Mr. Heygate once more: "It is scarcely too much to say that there was almost a silence on the subjects of the Judgment, of the Church, of the Communion of Saints. The incarnation was only known in reference to the cross; the sacraments were reduced to the position of Judaic ordinances; the eucharistic sacrifice was unheard of; the intermediate state unrecognized; prayers for the departed scouted as a piece of popery, if ever mentioned; the sanctity of the body in consequence of the incarnation and of baptism was unthought of; worship as such had given place to supposed 'edification;' our Union with the Catholic Churches of Christendom was undreamed of."

As the arrangements of the pews were made with a view to accommodate people comfortably while they sat and listened, and little care taken that they might kneel and pray—so little was taught from the pulpit as to the solemnity and importance of a devotional life. The grand object of the gathering was to hear a sententious, dry, and formal discourse from an orthodox preacher, or an eloquent and powerful declamation on the doctrine of the cross from an evangelical. In fact the fortunes of the church as a spiritual society taken as a whole were at their lowest ebb.

We must not, however, conclude that God had left Himself altogether without witness. There was a certain measure of zeal and earnestness after the teaching of Wesley, working outside the pale of the establishment but to some extent acting upon her. In such an age it might well be wild, reckless, and ungovernable in the absence of hands capable of holding the reins. But within the pale of the Holy Fold were a multitude of earnest, humble, sober-mined Christian people scattered about over the country, leavening the whole and saving it from corruption.

There was not the organisation, the inter-communication and the self-advertisement which we have witnessed in later years. Pious Christian ladies were content with the sphere afforded for their exertions by the ignorance or poverty of their own rural parishes, and never dreamed of appearing on the platform in the county town or in London.

The press did not teem then, as now, with a multitude of devotional booklets of every shade of opinion, but the spiritual life of "the faithful who were not famous" was nourished chiefly on the writings of the great fathers of the evangelical succession, at the leaders among whom we must briefly glance as the men who had formed the religious tone of the country in the early years of the century, and on whose teachings the souls and minds of the great leaders of the Tractarian movement had been trained.

Of this school the four great evangelists were John Newton, Thomas Scott, Joseph Milner, and Henry Venn. Newton was regarded as the great living example of the spiritual power of the principles of the evangelical system to redeem and save. Scott was their great interpreter of Holy scripture, Milner their ecclesiastical historian, and Venn their systematic teacher of the duties and the faith of the Christian life. Of all four Sir J. Stephen has written excellently, and it is to his pages that we have mainly turned for information respecting them.

John Newton's life was spread over the greater part of the eighteenth century. At twelve years of age he began a seafaring life in a merchant vessel under the command of his father. His mother was then dead, but had flung along her young son's future path the safeguard of many prayers. As often happens in the case of those whose earlier years have been affected by the strong and persistent application of religious influences, John Newton fluctuated strangely between piety and carelessness. "I took up," he says, "and laid aside a religious profession, three or four times before I was sixteen years old. I spent the greater part of every day in reading the scriptures, in meditation, and in prayer. I fasted often; I even abstained from animal food for three months. I would hardly answer a question, for fear of speaking an idle word."

From this state of mind Newton passed to scepticism, and thence to a state of abandoned sensuality. We see him pressed into the king's service, and gather that the discipline of H.M. ship "Harwich," though deeply abhorrent to him, was not altogether unprofitable. Then we find him overseer of a slave depot on the Gold Coast, and anon wandering along the pestilential shore with no solace but a copy of Barrow's Euclid, the diagrams of which he would trace on the sand, finding an escape from trouble in the satisfaction of geometrical truth. At last he was rescued by a Liverpool ship and brought back to England. Subsequently, as commander of a slave ship he made four voyages to the African coast, and was then compelled, by illness, to exchange his seafaring life for the office of a landing waiter in the Customs at Liverpool.

But another more momentous change was to be his. It had been his mother's cherished hope that he might become a faithful minister of Christ's gospel, and that hope received at last a tardy, but most ample fulfilment. Gradually a taste for the Bible and for books of devotion expelled all other literature from his cabin. "Old ocean probably never before or since floated such another slave ship. On board of her, indeed, were to to be seen all the ordinary phenomena. Packed together like herrings, stifled, sick, and broken-hearted, the negroes in that aquatic Pandemonium died after making futile attemps at insurrection. But, separated by a single plank from his victims, the voice of their gaoler might be heard, day by day, conducting the prayers of his ship's company, singing a devout imitation of his own of the verses of Propertius ('*tu mihi curarum requies*' etc.), and, as he assures us, experiencing on his last voyage to Guinea sweeter and more frequent hours of divine communion than he had ever elsewhere known."

A strange training this for a ministry of special power in later years, yet true as strange. After some wavering between the Church and Nonconformity he was ordained, in his thirty-ninth year, as a Deacon of the Church of England, and curate of the parish of Olney, in Buckinghamshire; his one solicitude being to find "a public opportunity to testify the riches of Divine grace, thinking that he was, above most living, a fit person to proclaim that faithful saying, that Christ Jesus came into the world to save the chief of sinners."

At Olney, Newton composed and published many sermons and letters, of which the best known volume is the *Cardiphonia*, an expression of the utterance of the heart in the form of religious correspondence—a work which half-a-century ago would have an honoured place on the shelves of almost every religious household. The portrait on the first page of the present writer's copy represents Newton as a heavy, kindly-looking man, just in his element in the full white wig, the preacher's gown, and the ample white bands of the period.

At Olney, Newton formed that friendship which the genius of Cowper has immortalised, and there, too, he exercised a deep influence on the spiritual training of Thomas Scott, the commentator, but his own pastoral labours in that obscure corner of the vineyard were not rewarded with any conspicuous measure of success. Eventually he became rector of St. Mary Woolnoth, in the City of London, where he continued till his death in 1807, at the age of eighty-two. We have lingered for a few lines over Newton's honoured name; for, himself the spiritual child of Whitfield, whom he met in America, "he was one of the spiritual progenitors of Claudius Buchanan, to whom the Church of India owes so large a debt of gratitude, of William Wilberforce, to whom the Church universal is still more largely indebted; of Joseph Milner, whom he induced to write the "History of the Church" of ancient times, and of Thomas Scott, who has bequeathed to the Church, in ages yet to come, writings of imperishable value, and the memory of a life passed in no unsuccessful emulation of those of whom this unhallowed world was the least worthy."

The name of Thomas Scott, the spiritual son of Newton is, it may be, little more than a name to the religious world of the present day; yet be it remembered that John Henry Newman has written these words in his *Apologia* : " The writer who made a deeper impression on my mind than any other, and to whom (humanly speaking) I almost owe my soul—Thomas Scott, of Aston, Sandford. I so admired and delighted in his writings, that, when I was an undergraduate, I thought of making a visit to his Parsonage, in order to see a man whom I so deeply revered." . . . . . " I hung upon the lips of Daniel Wilson, afterwards Bishop of Calcutta, as in two sermons at St. John's Chapel he gave the history of Scott's life and death. I had been possessed of his *Force of Truth*, and essays, from a boy; his Commentary I bought when I was an undergraduate."

The history of Scott's life in fine was as follows, " The tenth child of a grazier in Lincolnshire, he was born in 1747. After passing five years at the grammar-school at Scorton, in that county, he was apprenticed to a medical man. Being dismissed from that service for gross misconduct he returned home at the age of sixteen, and passed the nine following years in 'the most laborious and dirty parts of the grazier's business.' Then to escape a lifetime of menial employment he applied himself with vigour to regain and enlarge his well-nigh forgotten knowledge of Latin and Greek. At the age of twenty-six he was ordained deacon, and after passing more than thirteen years as curate of various parishes in Buckinghamshire (Olney amongst the rest), he was then appointed to a hospital chapel in Grosvenor Place, where he worked for seventeen years. He was presented in 1803 to the rectory of Ashton Sandford, and died there in April, 1821. "He died unknown or unheeded by the poets, the philosophers, the historians, and the artists, who, during the same momentous era, had established an intellectual sovereignty in his native land." . . . . . "He died neglected, if not despised, by the hierarchy of the Church of England." "But he died amidst the regrets, and yet lives in the grateful remembrance, of numbers without number, who, on either side of the Atlantic (in Continental, as well as in insular Britain), had founded in his writings such a mass of diversified instruction, such stores of intellectual and spiritual nutriment, such completeness and maturity of divine knowledge, so steady and so pure a light to lighten the dark places of Holy Scripture, so absolute a devotedness to truth, and so indefatigable a pursuit of truth, as they had not found in any or in all of the theologians who wrote or spake in his own times, and in his own mother tongue."

In *The Force of Truth,* Scott has recorded the history of his search for truth during three successive years in retirement and almost in solitude. "The Bible lay continually open on his table. Day by day, and hour by hour, he implored the Divine Author of it to become also the infallible interpreter. From page to page, and from sentence to sentence, he searched, weighed, and collated every word with unremitting diligence and inextinguishable ardour." The same method, the same care, the same diligence were employed by him in the production of his great Commentary on the Bible which formed the magnum opus of his life. The six quarto volumes of which it consists can hardly compete successfully with the productions of Wordsworth, Alford, Ellicott, and that host of modern Commentators, who have equipped themselves for their arduous task with the full panoply of critical and exegetical apparatus supplied by the learned investigation of recent years; but they may well be preserved in many a quiet parsonage for a decade or two longer, as one of the more interesting memorials of the religious life of the earliest years of the century now drawing towards its close.

"The saturation of the comment by the spirit of the text is the true and characteristic merit of Mr. Scott's *exegesis.*" And the saturation of his own life by the same spirit was the prime cause of the spiritual vitality of many of his works. "He was a poor and even a necessitous man." We find him "under the accumulated burdens of sixty-seven years, of sickness, and of poverty, investigating his accounts, and ascertaining that £199,900 had been paid in his life time across the counter for his theological publications—that he had himself derived from them an income of a little more than £47 per annum—that they had involved him in a debt of about £1,200—and that all his worldly wealth consisted of a warehouse full of unsaleable theology." "His annual income, professional and literary, seldom approached £200, and usually amounted to but half that sum," but "he lived in severe frugality, in brave independence, and in a self-denying charity to those who were still poorer than himself."

Can we wonder that the spirit of such a writer and such a man flashed up into fresh life in the young soul of such an one as John Henry Newman. The religious history of the race does not afford many instances of the influence of a nobler teacher over a nobler pupil.

Nor can we on this page omit all mention of Joseph Milner, Master of the Grammar School at Hull, and one of the ministers of the High Church in that town. He was, as we have observed, the ecclesiastical historian of the Evangelical party, and he set himself to demonstrate in his "History of the Church of Christ" that "from the days of Peter and of Paul, there had been an unbroken succession of Christian teachers, and of Christian societies among whom the eternal fire of gospel truth had burnt pure and undefiled by the errors which were abjured in the sixteenth century by the half of Christendom."

Though it be the opinion of the most competent judges that Milner failed to establish the theory to which he was pledged, still he unquestionably succeeded in showing that the religion of English Evangelical Churchmen had existed substantially, if not formally, in the souls of a long succession of saints, reaching backwards from the age of the great European Reformation to the first century of the Christian era.

To Henry Venn also a word of notice must be accorded. In the "*Complete* Duty of Man," he set himself to remedy the defects and to reject the false premises of the "Whole Duty of Man." Venn's work is "still one of those few books of which the benefits are never unfelt, of which the love never abates, and of which the republication is never long intermitted." . . . "He might have borrowed for this, and for all his writings, from his friend John Newton, the title of Cardiphonia."

In the early years of the century, however, there were two or three considerable figures in the religious world whose influence was of a personal and social rather than of an intellectual or literary kind.

Wilberforce, the great leader of the Clapham sect, was devoting every energy to the abolition of the slave trade, and the purification of social manners and customs. And the influence exercised in the House of Commons by the wealthy and earnest Member for Yorkshire was probably greater than any which fell to him as the author of the *Practical View*.

Meanwhile Isaac Milner, Dean of Carlisle, and President of Queen's College, Cambridge, occupied a unique position in the religious world of the day.

"Under the shelter of his name, his college flourished as the best cultured and most fruitful nursery of the evangelical neophytes of Cambridge. From a theological school maintained at Elland, in Yorkshire, at the charge of the Clapham exchequer, an unbroken succession of students were annually received there; destined, at the close of their academical career, to ascend and animate the pulpits of the national church."

Last, but in some ways the most considerable among

our list of worthies, stands the figure of Charles Simeon, an Etonian, and then a Fellow of King's College, Cambridge, and minister of Holy Trinity Church in that town. This great and good man was unquestionably subject to many an unbecoming foible, and candid friends could hardly acquit him of the charge of coxcombry, but in spite of all weaknesses, the broad fact remains that in the Church of Holy Trinity there gathered every Sunday, for more than half a century, "a crowd which hung on the lips of the preacher, as men hearken to some unexpected intelligence of a deep but ever varying interest," and "towards the close of that long period, the pulpit of St. Mary's was, occasionally, the centre of the same attraction, and with a still more impressive result."

During all these years young men who had come under the influence, that strangely powerful personality at the most receptive period of their lives, were going forth to proclaim throughout England the same spiritual truths which they had learned from Charles Simeon's lips. As often happens, however, the disciples failed to approximate very closely to the spirit and power of the master; and while it required the genius and earnestness of Simeon to make his sermon skeletons tolerable to his hearers, the Simeon-and-water discourses inflicted on many a rural congregation were hardly good to the use of edifying.

Meanwhile, various causes were tending to destroy the influence of the Church in the popular estimate.

The works of Cobbett, teeming with furious invective against the abuses of the Establishment, were circulated in immense numbers, chiefly among the poorer classes, and containing as they did much truth, and much sound common sense, though mixed with much sophistry and falsehood, resulted in the strengthening of popular feeling against the Church.

Much of the tithe, moreover, was at that time levied in kind, and was a source of constant irritation between the clergy and the farmers.

The orthodox High Church Clergy had almost unanimously opposed the abolition of the slave trade, and had thus lost the respect of many of the most enlightened members of all classes.

A government, which professed to be liberal, was apparently, mutilating while it professed to reform the position of the Church. The Bishoprics were swept away from the Irish Church at one fell swoop, a measure which, however deserved and just it might be, could not fail to exasperate and intensify party feeling; even the English Bishops themselves were told by the Premier, Lord Grey, to "set their houses in order," and the noble lord was reported to have said privately that the Church was a mare's nest. The Press teemed with publications demanding alterations in the Prayer Book, for the sake of accommodating infidels and dissenters. Even Dr. Arnold imagined that the churches might with advantage be used by the various dissenting bodies in turn.

The mass of the clergy, true to their invariable policy, resisted every attempt that was made to effect reforms, which were generally regarded as at once righteous and inevitable, "insomuch that if the Government which came into power in the year 1830, and brought in the great Reform Bill, had at that time proposed the disestablishment of the Church, the measure would probably have been carried at that moment with very little opposition."

CHAPTER II.

THE "WHERE"—ORIEL COLLEGE, OXFORD

OF the four-and-twenty Oxford Colleges, Oriel was, during the first forty years of this century, unquestionably the most prominent. In the intellectual history of the University it competed up to the years 1830 or 1835 on at least equal terms with Balliol, while, as regarded ecclesiastical and spiritual influence, it took an easy lead of all the rest.

The etymology of the word Oriel has been much discussed; some have understood it as implying "The Lion, or the Light, or the Altar of God;" but it is, perhaps, most correctly derived from the mediæval word *oriolum*, meaning porch or gateway, or rather the room over the porch or gateway, which often contained a small chapel or oratory. "It is supposed that an ancient chapel once stood here, belonging to a chaplain of Queen Eleanor of Castile, and called *La Oriole*. A story says that Edward the second, flying from the field of Bannockburn, vowed that he would found a religious house in honour of the Virgin if ever he returned in safety. He performed his vows, and traces of his original foundation still remain in a certain groined crypt, and some arches. Edward III. gave the present site, which belonged to his mother's chaplain; and hence it explained the frequent appearance of the Spanish pomegranates among the college decorations."

Oriel numbers in the beadroll of its sons the illustrious names of Sir Walter Raleigh and Bishop Butler; but in modern times the names of Whately, Pusey, Newman

R. H. Froude, Arnold, Wilberforce, Keble, and Fraser, have given it a lustre which may have become dimmed, but which will never be forgotten.

Dr. Burgon, the present Dean of Chichester, writing more than twenty years ago of the old Foundation, with which he was so long connected as a Fellow, thus described the causes which brought about the dawn of Oriel's great day :—" The visitor whose curiosity has been excited by its present fame, gazes with disappointment on a collection of buildings which have with them so few of the circumstances of dignity or wealth. Broad quadrangles, high halls and chambers, ornamented cloisters, stately walks or umbrageous gardens, a throng of students, ample revenues, or a glorious history—none of these things were the portion of that foundation; nothing, in short, which to the common eye, sixty years ago, would have given tokens of what it was to be. But it had at that time a spirit working within it which enabled its inmates to do, amid its seeming insignificance, what no other body in the place could equal—not a very abstruse gift or extraordinary boast, but a rare one— the honest purpose to administer the trust committed to them in such a way as their conscience pointed out best. So, whereas the colleges of Oxford are self-electing bodies, the Fellows in each perpetually filling up from among themselves the vacancies which occur in their number, the members of this foundation determined, at a time when, either from evil custom or from ancient statute, such a thing was not known elsewhere, to throw open their fellowship to the competition of all comers, and, in the choice of associates, henceforth to cast to the winds every personal motive and feeling, family connection, and friendship, and patronage, and political interest, and local claim, and prejudice, and party jealousy, and to elect solely on public and patriotic grounds. Nay, with a remarkable independence of mind, they resolved that even the table of honours, awarded to literary merit by the University in its new system of examination for degrees, should not fetter their judgment as electors, but that, at all risks, and whatever criticism it might cause, and whatever odium they might incur, they would select the men, whoever they were, to be children of their founder, whom they thought, in their consciences, to be most likely, from their intellectual and moral qualities, to please him if (as they expressed it) he were still upon earth; most likely to do honour to his college; most likely to promote the objects which they believed he had at heart."

To Dr. Eveleigh, who was provost of Oriel from 1781 down to 1814, and whom Keble describes as "a man to bring down a blessing upon any society of which he was a member," belongs the honour of originating the statute prescribing the public examinations and the Honour Lists, which rapidly lifted the university, as a place of education, out of the prostrate condition in which it had lain for more than a century. He, too, was the prime mover of the reform in the method of election to the Oriel Fellowships which Dr. Burgon has described, and by the beginning of the century had gathered round him a body of able subordinates selected from the university at large, on the ground of intellectual or moral qualification alone. Such a body of men would naturally desire to co-optate associates of the same calibre and tastes as their own, and the principle of "like chooses like" became as useful in the case of Oriel as it had been mischievous in other common rooms, where the colleges had been looked upon in the light of private clubs, into which only clubable men had any right of admission.

"For nearly thirty years the examinations for Oriel Fellowships were conducted upon the principle of ascertaining, not what a man had read, but what he was like. The prizes or classes which a candidate might bring with him to the competition were wholly disregarded by the electors, who looked at his papers unbiassed by opinion outside. The verdict of the university examiners was not only often set aside, but even outraged. If Keble, Hawkins, and Jenkyns were double-firsts, Whately, T. Mozley, Newman, and Hurrell Froude were all men of low classes, and taken against candidates of greater *primâ facie* claims. Perhaps the word which best expresses what was looked for in the papers of the candidates for an Oriel Fellowship is—originality."

Such was the work originated by Eveleigh, and completed by Dr. Copleston, who succeeded him as Provost in 1814, and held the office until his translation in 1827 to the Deanery of St. Paul's and the Bishopric of Llandaff.

Copleston remains a very considerable figure in the literary history of that time, his name being then well-known outside Oxford as a regular contributor to the *Quarterly Review*, and an able writer on questions of currency and finance. Within the University he enjoyed an assured ascendency as its champion against the attacks of the *Edinburgh Review*, and within the walls of Oriel he was all-powerful, the Headship being pressed upon him in 1814 in an address signed by all the fellows. Mr. Mozley, who entered the college in 1822, knew Copleston as "the most substantial and majestic, and, if I may say so, richly-coloured character within my knowledge;" and has also described the richness and melody of Copleston's voice as surpassing any instrument. "No one who had only heard him take his part in the Communion service could ever forget the tone. It penetrated everybody, entered into the soul, and carrying with it much of the man himself, made the least thing he said adhere to the memory and be easily producible."

In 1829, Dr. Hawkins, mainly through Newman's support, was elected Provost of Oriel in succession to Copleston, and it had been said by Mr. Mozley in reference to this—" Voice must have had no small part in Hawkins' election to the Provostship. His was a remarkable combination of sweetness with strength, sincerity, seriousness and decision." On reaching this position he entered upon an inheritance, fraught with most serious anxieties, but rich in most glorious potentialities.

For many years during the Copleston *régime* a most profound influence, mental and spiritual, had been exercised in the College and University by Whately, one of the tutors, afterwards widely known as Archbishop of Dublin, originally a disciple of Copleston—but a disciple by whom the master was soon content to be represented, not to say personated. Whately stood alone and self-sufficient on a lofty eminence of free speculation, regarding High Church and Low Church as equal bigotries, with a certain respect for the best representatives of the former as learned and cultivated men, but ignoring the system of the latter—at least that side of it presented there at Oxford—as below contempt. "For Whately was claimed by his admirers a spiritual as well as mental pre-eminence, but it would not be possible to describe now the terror his presence was sure to infuse among all who wished things to remain much as they were in their own lifetime. Instead of being comforted and built up in the good old fashion, they were told they were altogether wrong, and must first retrace all their steps and undo all they had been doing. What was worse, the efficacy of the cure which had become necessary consisted in the hearers thinking it out for themselves."

It would have been easy to predict that the influence of such a master mind upon a number of the most talented young men in the University, meeting and dining together day by day, would certainly result in the shaking of old beliefs, and in a general unsettlement of opinion; it would have been equally impossible to prophecy where those who were then shaken from their old moorings would ultimately drift. Containing as the college did some of the most vigorous minds, and the most attractive characters in Oxford, it became a matter of grave importance that its most prominent talkers should seem " to be always undermining, if not actually demolishing, received traditions and institutions; and whether they were preaching from the University pulpit, or arguing in common room, or issuing pamphlets on passing occasions, even faithful and self-reliant men felt the ground shaking under them. The new Oriel set was declared to be Noetic, whatever that may mean, and when a Fellow of the College presented himself in the social gatherings of another society, he was sure to be reminded of his pretence to intellectual superiority."

To quote from another writer,—" The Noetics knew nothing of the philosophical movement which was taking place on the Continent; they were imbued neither with Kant nor with Rousseau, yet this knot of Oriel men was distinctly the product of the French Revolution. They called everything in question; they appealed to first principles, and disallowed authority as a judge in intellectual matters." .... "It was the men in whom this disposition reigned in Oriel that gave the college its celebrity in the country. The most known names were, besides Provost Copleston, Whately, Arnold, Hampden, Baden Powell. Blanco White, though only an honorary member of the college, lived much in the common-room."

Into such a society, such an atmosphere, and into a common-room, which "stank of logic" were John Keble, John Henry Newman, Edward Bouverie Pusey, and Richard Hurrell Froude, introduced prior to the year 1827 in which Hawkins was called to the headship.

They were hardly men to be content with mere negations, or as Stanley was once said to be, with a theology whose only unity and completeness was that of a landscape covered with mist. R. H. Froude was a bold rider both in speculation and on horseback, and was essentially a man "not afraid of inferences." J. H. Newman has recorded how Dr. Whately "emphatically, opened my mind, and taught me to think, and to use my reason," but he goes on a few lines further—"After a few years had passed, I began to believe that his influence on me in a higher respect than intellectual advance (I will not say through his faults), had not been satisfactory."

Over such a society then was Dr. Hawkins called to rule, a society gathering round a tea-pot which was for more than a generation the centre of intellectual activity, and of religious and philosophical thought and speculation. For it may be mentioned here, to their eternal honour, that the Fellows of Oriel were the first to abandon that excessive use of wine which continued to degrade the upper ranks of English society until a period within the memory of living persons.

This was the first common room in which tea was drunk, and in the year 1825, "one of the first standing jokes against the College, all over the University, was the Oriel tea-pot, supposed to be always ready; the centre of the Oriel circle, and its special inspiration."

At such a juncture, " A man of wide sympathies, and the power of guiding and ruling others, which so often springs from wide sympathies, might have turned such materials to the best account, and have used the exceptional zeal and talents of the staff from whom he had to select for the maintenance of the high character and traditions of the College; but such a man in those years was not forthcoming. Dr. Hawkins, the Provost, was a fine scholar and a high-bred gentleman ; but of cold temperament, and stiff and punctilious in manners ; a high and dry churchman of the old school, very methodical, very conservative, who looked even on his old friend Arnold with some misgiving and was entirely out of sympathy with those who were now turning the academical and religious world upside down." Such is the estimate of Dr. Hawkins formed by Mr. Thos. Hughes, and recorded by him in connection with the election to an Oriel Fellowship in 1840 of James Fraser, afterwards so widely known as the popular Bishop of Manchester. This estimate of the Provost of Oriel is not directly contradicted by what Dr. Newman, whose opinion on this point carries at least as great weight as that of Mr. Hughes, has placed on record. "When I took orders in 1824, and had a curacy in Oxford, then, during the long vacations, I was especially thrown into his company. I can say with a full heart that I love him, and have never ceased to love him ; and I thus preface what might otherwise sound rude, that in the course of the many years in which we were together afterwards, he provoked me very much from time to time, though I am perfectly certain that I have provoked him a great deal more. Moreover, in me such provocation was unbecoming, both because he was the Head of my College, and because, in the first years that I knew him, he had been in many ways of great service to my mind."

He was the first who taught me to weigh my words, and to be cautious in my statements. He led me to that mode of limiting and clearing my sense in discussion and in controversy, and of distinguishing between cognate ideas, and of avoiding mistakes by anticipation, which to my surprise has been since considered, even in quarters friendly to me, to savour of the polemics of Rome. He is a man of most exact mind himself, and he used to snub me severely, on reading, as he was kind enough to do, the first sermons that I wrote, and other compositions which I was engaged upon."

Nor again is Mr. Hughes' verdict directly contravened by what Mr. Mozley says about Hawkins in connection with his election to the Headship. " Hawkins, who had long striven to keep an even course between all sides, had really won the love and esteem of all. In whatever he wrote or said, he laboured to concede to anyone what he asked, without sacrificing what was due to the truth, as he conceived it. He spoke incisively, and what he said remained in the memory and seemed to come from him. He was fond of business *and wished to keep it in his own hands.*" The italics of the last sentence are our own; it goes to show why men of first-rate ability, like Newman and R. H. Froude, could not long work under him.

Anyhow, at the time of the election, "university opinion pronounced that the headship lay between Keble and

Hawkins, and when Hawkins, by Newman's support, obtained the prize, it was not denied that the college had made a proper choice," for, as Mr. Mark Pattison tells us, "The new Provost was not, indeed, the equal of Keble, either in nobility of character or in literary power. But Hawkins was superior to Keble in some of those more superficial qualities which recommend a man as a head of a college—in ready tact, in aptitude for the small details of administration, and strict attention to the enforcement of college rules. Hawkins was, I suppose, generally the more practical man of the two."

"You don't know Hawkins as well as I do," wrote an old Oriel fellow to Newman after the election; "he will be sure to disappoint you."

Anyhow, "Within five years of Hawkins' election, Oriel showed symptoms of having begun to decline," but "up to 1830 there were no visible symptoms of dissatisfaction in the College, though everyone must have felt the thinness and superficiality of the new Provost's character by contrast with the sterling force and richness of that of his predecessors."

"The tutors of the College in 1830 were Newman, Hurrell Froude, Robert Wilberforce—all of them considered to be amongst the most rising men in the University. They were bestowing on their pupils as much time and trouble as is usually only expected from very good private tutors, and in return the tutors were rewarded by the enthusiastic following of no inconsiderable band of admiring disciples." In this year, however, two of the three tutors, Newman and Froude, proposed to the Provost some improvements in the usual course of instruction provided by the College. Hawkins received the proposal with dismay, thinking that, under the new scheme the tutors would get the tuition, and consequently the conduct of the College into their own hands; and that, in the event of their constantly introducing fresh books, the Provost would either have to be at the pains of getting those books up himself, or would find himself unable to take his part as heretofore in the College examinations. In addition to this difficulty the situation was aggravated by Newman's insistence on regarding his relation to his pupils as a pastoral one. He could not sink the functions of the priest in those of the tutor. Hence his scheme involved the entering of his share of the undergraduates under him, and the rest in due proportions under the other tutors. This point Newman would not give up, and as it interfered with the Provost's proposal that all the undergraduates should be entered under one common name, the tutor resigned, or rather was turned out, and Froude went with him.

"It is clear that, under the system for which Newman contended, a college must have become a mere priestly seminary and not an agent of a university." If it happened as T. Mozley relates, we must infer that "a narrow collegiate jealousy on the part of the Head prevailed with him to sacrifice what he saw to be the interest of the college to the maintenance of his own authority. He would not do this consciously; he would be impressed with the view that, the welfare of the college being dependent on the Head, the Head must, before all things, be supreme in all that regards the tuition."

In the above paragraph Mr. Pattison appears somewhat self-contradictory, for Hawkins cannot be justly accused of narrow collegiate jealousy in resisting changes which would turn the college into a mere priestly seminary. The upshot of the matter, however was simply this, that Froude and Newman being released from the systematic work of the tutorial office, and consequently with more leisure on their hands, gave greater attention than heretofore to the investigation of theological questions, to observations of the signs of the times, and to the exercises of personal self-discipline or the spiritual instruction of others; Froude was setting an example of most strict asceticism, while Newman, after serving the curacy of S. Clements, was now Vicar of Great S. Mary's, and already beginning to be known as one of the preachers of the day.

CHAPTER III.

THE "BY WHOM."

A BRIEF controversy has lately taken place in the columns of the *Guardian*, between Professor Stokes and the present Dean of St. Paul's, upon the question of the true paternity of the "Tractarian Movement." The former contributed an article to the August number of the *Contemporary Review*, in which he set himself to demonstrate that "Wesley begat Knox, and Knox begat Jebb, and Jebb begat Rose, and Pusey and Newman." To this article Dean Church replied—"Mr. Keble Mr. R. H. Froude, Mr. Newman, Dr. Pusey were the persons, who, as a matter of fact, were the authors and leaders of the 'Tractarian Movement.' In their minds its characteristic ideas took shape. In their conviction and enthusiasm it began its course. In their guidance were the steps and measures of its advance. They wrote a great deal, and a great deal has been written about them. What they said was definite enough ; the ground which they took was clearly marked ; they professed to revive and restore, and therefore they made a great point of having authority behind them, and of appealing to that mass of testimony in English Divinity and English practical religion which, as they believed, sanctioned their teaching."

Dean Church is no doubt substantially correct in this statement of the origin of the movement, if we except the one clause—"What they said was definite enough ; the ground which they took was clearly marked."

The reader of Newman's *Apologia* can hardly accept this claim of definiteness and clearness, except in the sense that Dr. Newman's views, while a priest of the English Church, very definitely changed as time went on, and that the ground which he occupied in 1844 was clearly marked outside that where he had stood in 1834. No doubt there was substantial agreement among the leaders for some time, and they would naturally be driven to minimize any differences which might exist by the pressure of the most bitter and determined opposition which their great crusade provoked. Mr. R. H. Froude left as a characteristic instruction for his younger brothers that if ever they found Newman and Keble differing upon any vital point, they might venture to think for themselves.

Dean Church, however, admits up to a certain point Professor Stokes' contention that Knox had a share in promoting the Anglo-Catholic movement, and tells us how " Mr. Knox was an invalid and a recluse, and he passed his days in Ireland. The Irish Church, in the midst of a prevailing, and, for the most part very ignorant and oppressive Ultra-Protestantism, had a small band of divines who might hold their own with the most learned and ablest of their English contemporaries. Bishop Mant and Bishop Jebb kept up the standard of Churchmanship in the face of Calvinistic extravagance and intolerance; Mr. Archer Butler and Dr. Todd were men of even higher mark—one for intellectual force and the other for large and sound erudition; and to Mr. Palmer, translated from Ireland to Oxford, English Theology owes its first adequate work on Liturgies, and its first scholastic treatise on the Church. And certainly among the laymen who at the same period gave their attention to theology, no one could be named in the same breath with Mr. Knox. . . . .

"In an age of much conventionality, and much confident and superficial dogmatism, Mr. Knox takes us by surprise by the boldness and freedom, and at the same time the deep piety and reverence, of his independent position. How he could have come to his special opinions, how he could have dared to proclaim and assert them, with such intolerant prejudice all around him, is a continual wonder."

Dr. Church goes on to show how Knox was at one period of his life under Wesley's influence, and was probably impressed by him with opinions about the Sacraments and the discipline of the Church, which are not usually held by Wesleyans now. He also allows that Knox was professing, explaining, and defending views which afterwards came to be regarded as notes of the Oxford Movement, though Knox himself passed away in 1831, before the movement fairly began.

He denies, however, that the true leaders of the movement were personally much influenced by Knox's writings, although those writings may have affected the atmosphere of English religious thought in such a way as to make Tractarianism more easy of acceptance to many than it would otherwise have been. He says that the reason why Knox did not influence the real leaders of the movement is not hard to find. "Mr. Knox was professedly an eclectic, who had worked out for himself, by his own private thought and speculation, what he accepted as sound and true. *Their* attitude was that of men who looked upon the Church as the divine depository of revealed truth, and who accepted and developed what they had received from the Church— the Church of their own communion first, and ultimately from the Church universal. He was a religious philosopher in his study, free to theorise as he thought fit ;

and they were missionaries with a call to remind an apathetic Church of forgotten certainties; and there was always in them a distrust of his manner of speculation, even when they were in general agreement with his conclusions."

Just so. . . . From Dr. Church's point of view: Those, however, who have not, like Dr. Church, been fellows of Oriel, may be inclined to ask why private speculation and enquiry should be predicated of Dublin, while the sanctity of a Divine Call is claimed for the little knot of students at Oxford. Unprejudiced people may even venture to think that truth was as likely to be successfully wooed by a philosopher who claimed to be nothing more, and who made, as he was justified in doing, philosophical enquiry the pursuit of his life, as by persons holding official positions, the immediate duties of which they felt justified in postponing to what appeared to them a higher work. Into this point, however, we shall enter at more length in a future chapter.

Dr. Church quotes with approval some words of Dr. Newman, who, speaking in 1839 of Mr. Knox, observes:—" Such is the prophecy of a calm and sagacious mind, whose writings are themselves no slight evidence of the intellectual and moral movements under consideration. In this respect he outstrips Scott and Coleridge, that he realizes his own position, and is an instance in rudiment of those great restorations which he foresaw in development. And while he shares with the eminent writers of the day the work of advancing what he anticipated, others, doubtless, in a similar seclusion from passing events, shared with him anticipations which they were not led to advance or even to record. . . . A much-venerated clergyman of the last generation—one of the most strenuous maintainers of ancient doctrines, and an energetic opponent of those who wished to carry our Church further than it had hitherto gone in the career of Protestantism—said, shortly before his death, to a friend of our own, 'Depend upon it, the day will come when these great doctrines, now buried (those connected with the Church), will be brought out to the light of day, and then the effect will be quite fearful!'"

In the same passage from Dr. Newman, which Dr. Church quotes, the great master of the movement goes on to describe it as the work not of two or three individuals, but of some unseen intangible influence. "It is not here or there; it has no progress, no causes, no fortunes; it is not a movement, it is a spirit, it is a spirit afloat, neither in the 'secret chamber' nor 'in the desert,' but everywhere. It is within us, rising up in the heart when it was least expected." . . . "Nothing can show more strikingly the truth of this representation than to refer to what may be called the theological history of the individuals who, whatever be their differences from one another on important or unimportant points, yet are associated together in the advocacy of the doctrine in question. Dr. Hook and Mr. Churton represent the High-Church dignitaries of the last generation; Mr Perceval, the Tory aristocracy; Mr. Keble is of the country clergy, and comes from valleys and woods, far removed both from notoriety and noise; Mr. Palmer and Mr. Todd are of Ireland; Dr. Pusey became what he is from among the Universities of Germany, and after a severe and tedious analysis of Arabic MSS. Mr. Dodsworth is said to have begun in the study of prophecy; Mr. Newman to have been much indebted to the friendship of Archbishop Whateley; Mr. Froude, if anyone gained his views for his own mind; others have passed over from Calvinism and kindred religions. . . . . . Where then is the common origin to which may be referred the present movement? What head of a sect is there? What search of opinions may be traced from mind to mind? They are one and all in their degree the organs of one sentiment, which has risen up simultaneously in many places very mysteriously."—(*British Critic*, April, 1839.)

In the above passage Mr. Newman very modestly deprecated any notion of the march of opinions from mind to mind, inasmuch as even at the time when he was writing, the younger disciples of the movement were being called Newmaniacs.

Dr. Newman's ascription of the movement to the working of an invisible spirit accords, though he would hardly appreciate the connection, with Mr. Mark Pattison's theory that the knot of Oriel men who produced it were the product of the French Revolution. Mr. Pattison had in view the revolt of the Oriel School against authority as a judge in intellectual matters. It is not difficult to see that the same spirit, seeking vent in another direction, would dispose men to a disturbance of the *status quo* in theological opinion and ecclesiastical arrangements.

In regard to Bishop Jebb, who is spoken of by Professor Stokes as the link between Knox and the Oxford leaders, considerable varieties of opinion have been held. Sir James Stephen has alluded to Jebb as "an elegant inquirer into the curiosities of theological literature," and as "a great master of parallelisms and contrasts." Dr. Church writes to the *Guardian* that "Bishop Jebb, though an excellent person, was hardly the teacher to convert men like Mr. Keble and Mr. Newman."

Possibly not; but still more weight must be attached to Jebb's writings than Dr. Church is willing to admit. Professor Stokes seems clearly to have established that, whatever Jebb's personal influence may have been, the effect of his writings was very marked and widely spread. In those portions of the *Tracts for the Times*, which treat of Baptismal Regeneration, the Eucharistic Sacrifice, the Christian Priesthood, and Apostolic Succession, the one Bishop of this century who is always quoted is Bishop Jebb.

In the life of Dr. Hook, the great Vicar of Leeds, there are frequent references to Jebb, all of which go to show the profound respect with which he was regarded by many of the leading authorities of the Church of England. It will be sufficient to cite one instance. On a certain day in October, 1830, Dr. Hook dined at Fulham with the Bishop of London, the only other guest being the Archbishop of Canterbury. In a letter to Mrs. Hook describing the dinner, the following passage occurs:—

"Things were going on smoothly after this, when, lo and behold! in a meek and gentle voice the Lord Archbishop challenged the poor priest to take a glass of wine, and the said priest was again overpowered: he spilt the wine, first on the table-cloth, then on his coat, and forgot to bow to his grace. Luckily 'Piety without Asceticism'" (title of a work by Bishop Jebb) "was named, and the very thought of his dear, kind, apostolical patron, the Bishop of Limerick, inspired the poor priest once more with courage. We all chanted the praises of the work; and then the poor priest was listened to with interest, as he could give the latest account of Ireland's best prelate. Indeed he could not help thinking that his grace the Metropolitan seemed to treat him with more respect, when he remembered, probably, that he, the said priest, was immortalised by being mentioned in 'Practical Theology,' as Bishop Jebb's friend."

Again Hook, writing in 1840, still speaks of Jebb as "My dear Gamaliel." In view of these facts we may leave Dr. Church's sneer about Jebb, though an excellent person, being hardly likely to convert men like Mr. Keble, to take care of itself.

Again, before passing on, we may notice that Dr Hook, writing to a friend in 1834, remarks—" I exhort you very earnestly to read the correspondence of Knox and Jebb, because it is a book well calculated to calm your mind at the present time, and to set one a-thinking in the right line." .... "On all these points the words of Knox and Jebb appear to me to be the words of soberness and truth."

It must be remembered that Dr. Hook, who thus acknowledges his indebtedness to Knox and Jebb, was himself numbered by Dr. Newman among the leaders of the movement; and that without the moral support of men like Hook outside Oxford, the Oriel Anglo-Catholics would have stood little chance of impressing their views upon the Church at large.

Mr. Molesworth, in his "History of the Church of England," has drawn attention to the fact that the celebrated Presbyterian, Edward Irving, had in 1825 adopted the doctrine of baptismal regeneration, and in a volume of lectures had pushed that doctrine to its logical consequences. Such a fact, however, has about as much bearing on the history of the Tractarian movement, as the facts, also recorded by Mr. Molesworth, of Dr. Molesworth having been the leading writer for the *Penny Sunday Reader*, and of the same divine having

THE TRACTARIAN UPHEAVAL.

drawn up an address to the Archbishop of Canterbury on the revival of Convocation. Whatever may have been the position and influence of Irving, and in certain quarters it would be hard to overrate them, it is certain that few Anglicans would turn to him for guidance as to the principles or doctrine of their own Church.

The works of the great leaders of the Oriel school are almost, if not entirely, devoid of all reference to the teaching of the prophet of the so-called Catholic Apostolic Church; indeed most of them would have regarded his advocacy of any given opinion in the light of a detriment rather than a support.

We shall therefore devote the remainder of this chapter to the illustrious triumvirate who practically divided the leadership of the greatest religious movement which this century has witnessed in England.

Three Oxford clergymen—John Keble, Richard Hurrell Froude, and John Henry Newman—who were all Fellows and Tutors of Oriel, who lived for many years on terms of the closest friendship with each other, who were in constant inter-communication, who together mapped out the plan of campaign, and unitedly laboured in its execution, beyond all question claim the first and the leading place in our short narrative.

When we consider in the following chapters the history of the course of the movement, a few words will be devoted to others who, at sundry times and in divers manners, rendered it effectual aid; notably to Hugh James Rose a Cambridge man, associated to some extent with the truimvirs in its initial stage, and to Edward Bouverie Pusey, who, though he does not appear to have joined them till after their work was fairly started, in later years afforded them the support of his great name, and assistance which no one but himself could so well have rendered.

John Keble was born on St. Mark's Day, 1792, at Fairford in Gloucestershire. He was the second child and the eldest son of the Rev. John Keble and Sarah Maule, the daughter of the Incumbent of Ringwood; three sisters and one brother completed the family circle. A few words must be said of his father. He was a good scholar, and a man of considerable ability, besides being a clergyman of exemplary piety. He alone educated his two sons up to their going to Oxford, and both of them obtained scholarships at Corpus Christi College at an unusually early age. John Keble, as an undergraduate, used to say that his father had never compelled him to study, and that he was taught only when he liked to learn—a method of tuition which could only have answered in the case of an exceptionally conscientious boy. Such John Keble certainly was—he was always spoken of by one of his god-fathers as John the good.

In December, 1806, when as yet four months short of fifteen, John Keble competed successfully for a scholarship at Corpus, of which college his father had formerly been a scholar and fellow. The Corpus scholarships, of that day, though not entirely open, were yet sufficiently so to invite much competition: their value, and still more the strictness and impartiality with which the examinations were conducted, insured a number of good candidates for each vacancy. The college was a very small establishment, consisting of twenty fellows, twenty scholars, four exhibitioners, and six gentlemen commoners. The tuition afforded to the undergraduates was exceptionally good, and the college won more than its proportionate share of university honours. John

Keble seems to have competed unsuccessfully for several university prizes before taking his earliest degree. His non-success was probably attributable to his extreme youth, and to the fact that he was concentrating his reading upon the subjects of the two great honour schools, in which he obtained the very rare distinction of a double-first in the Easter term of 1810. At first after taking his B.A. degree he proposed to stand for a fellowship at Magdalen, but the reputation he had now obtained put an end to any scheme of this kind, by opening to him the prospect of the great distinction of a fellowship at Oriel.

He was elected a probationer fellow there on the 20th of April, 1811, being then a few days short of completing his nineteenth year. Whately entered Oriel along with him, and they found Copleston as Provost and Davison as Tutor leading at that time that most distinguished society.

Keble's progress was now rapid. In 1812 he won the prizes for both the Batchelor's essays. This was an honour at that time unprecedented, and one which since then has been very seldom repeated.

Being resident for some time in Oxford, but holding no college office, he soon became engaged in private tuition, taking some of his pupils to the sea-side in South Devon during the long vacation. Keble entered, with quick relish, into the gaieties of Sidmouth and Torquay, where no one was better received than himself. No one, moreover, " seemed to enjoy more heartily the morning and evening parties, the concerts, and dances, which were frequent; the scenery and the society both found him impressionable, and as was natural they had their effect upon his poetical powers; he composed more often and better than he had ever done before."

Soon after his return to Oxford in December, 1813, he was appointed to the office of Examining Master from the following Michaelmas, and he set himself diligently to prepare for the work. He had great misgivings, as was to be expected in one at once so young and so modest; but, when the time for the exercise of his office arrived, the simplicity and kindness of his manner, his thorough acquaintance with the examination subjects, together with his entire freedom from self-display—a failing to which examiners have sometimes been liable—made him very effective and popular in the schools.

About the same time his thoughts were much occupied about his ordination. He considered, to quote his own words, that "the salvation of one soul is worth more than the framing of the Magna Charta of a thousand worlds," and that there cannot be, "even among the angels, a higher privilege that we can form an idea of, than the power of contributing to the everlasting happiness of our neighbour to be specially delegated and assigned to us by Almighty God."

He was ordained Deacon on Trinity Sunday, 1815, and Priest on Trinity Sunday, 1816, both by the Bishop of Oxford. Writing eleven years later to a friend, he says:—"To-day I have been to an ordination, for the first time since I was ordained myself, and I have almost made a vow to be present at one every year. I think it would do one a great deal of good, *like going back to one's native air after long intervals.*"

He did not exhibit outwardly any extraordinary or excessive devotion to his great calling in the commencement of his ministry, which consisted in the sole charge of two parishes, East Leach and Burthorpe, small and contiguous, for six weeks in the long vacation; nor did he find it necessary to give up his Oxford employments, or to decline the Tutorship at Oriel when called on to take it.

Keble used to ride to and fro from Oxford, and on Sunday used to dine at a cottager's, paying for his dinner, and charging them to provide nothing extra for him.

A sturdy Baptist shoemaker used to attend Burthorpe Church, stating as his reason that he there heard the Gospel.

Early in 1817 Keble for a time quitted Oxford, to work in Gloucestershire as his father's curate, but was recalled in the following year as College Tutor. Feeling though he did that he was thus diverted for a time from the proper ministerial work of his life, he yet thought that he was discharging a duty which he owed to Oriel

His biographer, Sir J. T. Coleridge, tells us that, in the exercise of the functions of this eminently responsible office, " he was diligent in preparing his lectures, and complains in some of his letters that he had no time for his own private reading. He attached himself affectionately to his pupils, and many of them attached themselves with equal warmth to him. His manner with them at lecture was perfectly simple and unpretending; if he was ignorant and unable to answer a question or explain a difficulty, there was no attempt at concealment; nor could any pupil fail to see that his well-doing was at least as great a cause of happiness to his tutor as to himself. Misbehaviour or idleness, it was obvious, gave him sincere pain. Intimacies, of course, did not always grow up from the intercourse of the pupil-room, or they might afterwards cease from separation and other causes; but some life-long friendships were so made."

Sir William Heathcote became one of his pupils, and

the bond then formed between them was never loosened. In after years Sir William, as patron of the living of Hursley, established Keble in the position, where the rulers of the Church were, to their shame, content to leave him.

It was in these years, especially during his wanderings in the vacations, that he was already beginning to compose those sacred poems which afterwards found a place in *The Christian Year* and the *Lyra Innocentium*. At the close of the Hilary Term in 1823 he resigned the tutorship, to return to pastoral work as curate of Southrop, a small parish very near his father's cure, where he was drawn, in no small degree, by a wish to be with his own family.

His father was now far advanced in years, and the health, too, of his sisters was a cause of frequent anxiety, and it was characteristic of Keble to prefer the obscurity of rural life, and the discipline of "the trivial round and the common task" to the discharge of the duties of a most conspicuous position in a great seat of learning.

On leaving Oriel, his pupils testified to their sense of the value of his services by a handsome present of plate, the more significant in days when such gifts were very unusual. It seems to show that Keble had reached the hearts as well as the intellects of his pupils, and was a thing to be justly proud of, though Keble managed to conceal it from some even of his most intimate friends.

To the village of Southrop several of his pupils followed him occasionally for long visits, among whom may be named Robert Wilberforce, Isaac Williams, and Hurrell Froude.

In the year 1824 the position of Archdeacon of

Barbadoes, a post then worth £2,000 a year was offered to Keble, who admits that he could not help being dazzled by the prospect, though he firmly declined in view of his father's increasing infirmities.

Early in the following year Keble's letters shew him beginning seriously to contemplate the publication of *The Christian Year*. Had he been left to follow his own judgment that work would probably have never seen the light, but his natural modesty had to yield ultimately to the pressure of all his friends. In the latter part of this same year he went for the first time as curate of Hursley in Hampshire, though he was obliged soon afterwards to return to Gloucestershire.

In June, 1827, *The Christian Year* came out, to meet at once with a success for which even his most appreciative friends were quite unprepared.

It ran rapidly through several editions, and its sale has kept up well ever since.

Within the first twenty-six years of its existence no fewer than 108,000 copies were issued in forty-three editions; and during the nine months immediately following Mr. Keble's death in 1866 seven editions were issued of 11,000 copies.

In 1827, many of Keble's friends would have gladly seen him contest with Dr. Hawkins the Provostship of Oriel, and it is certain that, in default of Hawkins, no other candidate would have had a chance against Keble. The modesty, however, of the latter held him back from pressing his claims, which in this case would have hardly carried the day, Newman's great influence having been cast into the opposite scale. In 1831, however, Keble was appointed to the vacant chair of the Poetry Professorship at Oxford, a post which, in accordance with the usual custom, he held for the next ten years. His own words in regard to the subject of his Professorship are not without interest :—" My notion is to consider poetry as a vent for overcharged feelings, or a full imagination, and so account for the various classes into which Poets naturally fall, by reference to the various objects which are apt to fill and overpower the mind, so as to require a sort of relief. Then there will come in a grand distinction between what I call primary and secondary poets ; the first *poetising* for their own relief, the second for any other reason."

Keble was appointed vicar of Hursley in 1836, and there he remained for the rest of his life, occasionally visiting Oxford, but maintaining by correspondence a close connection with Mr. Newman, Mr. R. H. Froude, Dr. Pusey, and the other leading spirits in the Anglo-Catholic movement. No question of importance ever arose without Mr. Keble being consulted, and there were thousands of disciples scattered throughout the country who thought that there could be no appeal to any higher earthly judgment when once the oracle of Hursley had spoken.

His reputation with the religious world outside the walls of Oxford was, of course, created and established by *The Christian Year*, a work published with a view to promote " a sober standard of feeling in matters of practical religion," and to assist persons in " bringing their own thoughts and feelings into more entire unison with those recommended and exemplified in the Prayer-Book."

In reference to this remarkable work, the late Dean Stanley wrote : " *The Christian Year* has taken its place —certainly for this generation—next to the Authorised Version and the Prayer-Book, far above the Homilies and the Articles. For one who would enforce an

THE TRACTARIAN UPHEAVAL. 53

argument, or defend a text, by quoting the Eleventh Article or the Homily on Charity, there are a hundred who would appeal to *The Christian Year*. And it has reached far beyond the limits of the Established Church. Wherever English religion spreads, there also is found this little volume.

"It is within the memory of the present writer that, on a Sunday, in the desert of Mount Sinai, where books were naturally of the fewest, of four British travellers—two of them were Scotsmen—it was found that three had, in their small travelling library, brought out with them *The Christian Year*." ... "In the Crimean War, some fanatical chaplain had opposed the introduction of *The Christian Year* into the hospitals; but by the next arrival from England was a whole cargo of *Christian Years* brought by the daughter of the greatest of Scottish divines, Dr. Chalmers."

As another slight instance of the universality of the appeal of *The Christian Year* to the religious feeling of every school of thought, the present writer may, perhaps, be permitted to mention that the copy lying before him, from the preface in which two quotations were made a few lines back, is valuable to him as a gift many years ago from the present Chairman of the London School Board, who will hardly be suspected by his many friends of any undue leaning to the principles of the Anglo-Catholic School.

Mr. Thackeray has told us how:—"*The Christian Year* was a book which appeared about that time. The son and the mother whispered it to each other with awe—Faint, very faint, and seldom in after life Pendennis heard that solemn Church music; but he always loved the remembrance of it, and of the times when it struck on his heart, and he walked over the fields full of hope and void of doubt, as the Church bells rang on Sunday morning."

Dean Stanley has also told us how " Keble, in the best sense of the word, was not a sacred but a secular poet." .... "Not George Herbert or Cowper, but Wordsworth, Scott, and perhaps more than all, Southey, are the English poets that kindled his flame, and coloured his diction." ... "The allusions to nature are even superabundantly inwoven with the most sacred subjects." .... "The exactness of the descriptions of Palestine have been noted and verified on the spot, as very few such descriptions ever have been." ... "Oxford, Bagley Wood, and the neighbourhood of Hursley, might, we are sure, be traced through hundreds of lines both in *The Christian Year* and the *Lyra Innocentium.*"

Much to the same effect Sir Jas. Stephen has written: —"The author of *The Christian Year*, like the author of the *Excursion*, inhabited a world in which the humblest objects and the most familiar incidents were symbolical of whatever is most elevated in things spiritual, and most remote from our experience in things invisible. In the tame suburbs, the dusty roads, and the busy streets of Oxford, Mr. Keble lived by imagination, not by sight. On every side they teemed for him with analogies and interpretations of the significance of her liturgical offices, of the mysteries of her priesthood, and of the temples erected by no human hands in the souls of her worshippers. When he transferred to the canvas the rich hues in which the sanctuary within the veil of common things was disclosed to his own eyes, he was accustomed to throw over the picture an atmosphere, which, however brilliant, was not seldom so hazy as to be almost impervious. What the Virgin Mother had been to the great painters of Italy, that the Anglican or Elizabethan Church became to him. Immaculate in conception, peerless in beauty, resplendent with every grace, she presented herself to him as a living personality to be loved and wooed, and as a divine impersonation to be adored and hymned." The same brilliant writer has also told us that Mr. Newman's theology "differed from that of Mr. Keble, as a substance in a solidified form differs from itself when in a gaseous form."

Mr. Keble's poetry may have sometimes been hazy, and the haze may have led to his overstepping, unconsciously at times, the narrow limits of his ecclesiastical theories. Dean Stanley has noticed how "*as a poet* he not only touched the great world of literature, but he also was a free-minded, free-speaking thinker." Mr. J. A. Froude in treating of Keble presents a curiously cognate thought. He reminds us how "Plato, in the dialogue of the Io, describes an ingenuous young Athenian searching desperately for some one who would teach him to be wise. Failing elsewhere he goes to the poets. Those, he thought, who could say such fine things in their verses would be able to tell him in prose what wisdom consisted in. Their conversation unfortunately proved as profitless as that of the philosophers; and the youth concluded that the poetry came from Divine inspiration, and that when off the sacred tripod they were but common men." Mr. Froude was probably right. Keble doubtless was greater as a poet than as a man, though we are far from denying him to have been most likely a more saintly person than nine English clergymen out of ten. Still his character had certain obvious limitations. "He was not far seeing, his mind moved in the groove of a single order of ideas. He couldnot place himself in the position of persons who disagreed with him, and thus he could never see the strong points of their arguments. Particular ways of thinking he dismissed as wicked, although in his summary condemnation he might be striking some of the ablest and most honest men in Europe. If he had not been Keble he would have been called (treason though it be to write the words) narrow-minded.

. . . . "To his immediate friends he was genial, affectionate, and possibly instructive, but he had no faculty for winning the unconverted. If he was not bigoted he was intensely prejudiced. If you did not agree with him there was something morally wrong with you, and your 'natural man' was provoked into resistance. To speak habitually with authority does not necessarily indicate an absence of humility, but does not encourage the growth of that quality."

. . . . "Keble was incapable of vanity in the vulgar sense. But there was a subtle self-sufficiency in him which has come out more distinctly in his school." Mr. J. A. Froude, whom we have just been quoting, tells us how Keble on a certain occasion made a call upon a family, one member of which had adopted Liberal opinions in theology, but learning that the black sheep was at home, refused to enter the house, and remained sitting in the porch, in imitation presumably of St. John's flight from the bath at Ephesus on account of the presence under the same roof of the heretic Corinthus.

Much to the same effect it has been said by Mr. Mozley, that though Hursley presented the most beautiful picture of English society that this century can show, the great poet of his church being there content to spend himself in those humble ministrations which noisy pulpit adventurers proclaim to be utterly beneath their notice, still there are inevitable drawbacks in any earthly position. "People felt, not unjustly, that Keble was, as it were, a little smothered in the embrace of a not very large-minded or open-minded section of the aristocracy." . . . . . "It was impossible not to feel that his sympathies were very one-sided, and not enlarged or corrected, so to speak, up to the actual state of things in the Church and in the world. Moreover, people who have found a quiet harbour and made up their minds to remain there, are not quite the best advisers for those who are still struggling with the currents and storms of life."

But, "Considering his world-wide fame, considering also his deep interest in the questions which agitated the ecclesiastical mind, and the respect in which on these questions he was held as an oracle by half the English clergy, there is something inexpressibly touching in the quiet unostentatious humility with which he contented himself with his limited sphere."

And lastly let it never be forgotten that John Henry Newman regarded Keble as the true author of the Oxford movement, and has described himself as ready to sink into the ground in self-abasement when Keble first took his hand on the day of his election to a fellowship at Oriel. Milman, too, the Dean of St. Paul's, one of the intellectual giants of that day, loved and admired Keble and regarded him as "strangely anybody else unlike anybody else."

Richard Hurrell Froude was the eldest son of the Venerable Robert H. Froude, Archdeacon of Totness, a clever, knowing, quick and handy man, and was born in the parsonage-house of Dartington, in the county of Devon, in 1803, on the Feast of the Annunciation. He was educated at Eton and Oxford, having previously had the great advantage, while at Ottery Free School, of living in the family of the Rev. George Coleridge His health was never robust, and, when about sixteen years of age, he had a dangerous illness, the consequences of which obliged him to leave school, and to submit for many months to the most troublesome restraints, and to be debarred from all the amusements and pleasures of his age. All this, in spite of a naturally impatient temper, he is said to have borne not only with patience and compliance, but with a cheerful sweetness which endeared him to all around him. He went to Eton in 1816, and came into residence at Oxford, as a commoner of Oriel College, in the spring of 1821. Oriel alone, of all the Oxford Colleges, in those days, sifted her commoners by an entrance examination. The examination did not directly bring in youths from good families, but as soon as it became understood that Oriel chose to be ' select," good families were anxious to get their sons into it. The Froudes were a Devonshire family of excellent standing, and Oriel was obviously the most suitable college for the Archdeacon's eldest son.

"As an undergraduate he waged a ruthless war against sophistry and loud talk, and he gibbeted one or two victims, labelling their sophisms with their names."

In 1824 he took his degree of B.A. obtaining high, though not the highest, honours, viz., a double-second class in the schools of Literæ Humaniores and of Disciplinæ Mathematicæ et Physicæ. At Easter, 1826 he was elected a Fellow of Oriel, and in 1827, accepted the office of Tutor, which he held as J. H. Newman's colleague till 1830, in which year they both retired in consequence of radical disagreements with Dr. Hawkins, the Provost. In December, 1828, he received Deacon's orders, and in the following year Priest's. The disorder which eventually terminated his life, first shewed itself in the summer of 1831. The winter of 1832-1833 he passed with Newman in the South of Europe, having been ordered off from the severity of the English winter; but "like most other Englishmen, he would not be indoors by sunset, or put on warmer clothing when the thermometer dropped twenty or thirty degrees. It happened to be an exceptionally cold winter in the Mediterranean. As far as regards health, the experiment had been a failure."

The two next winters, and the year between them (1832) were spent by him in the West Indies. He returned to England only to fade away, though the illness which immediately preceded his death lasted but a few weeks. He departed this life on the 28th of February, 1836, at his father's house at Dartington where he had been born.

It has been said by one eminently qualified to judge that if there could be any question as to the master spirit of the Tractarian movement, it lies between John Henry Newman and Richard Hurrell Froude. To middle-aged men now he is indeed little more than a mere *nominis umbra*, and owes the place, which he does hold in men's minds, in no slight degree, to the reputation gained since then by his younger brother, James Anthony Froude, the distinguished historian and essayist.

But sixty years ago, Richard Hurrell Froude was a Presence and a Power never to be ignored or forgotten by the circle of Oriel thinkers who were so deeply to influence the mind of England.

His character was a strangely complex one, and in forming a judgment of the contrarieties of his peculiarly gifted nature, we cannot do better than call his mother into Court, to speak of what he was in his earliest years.

She was a beautiful, highly-gifted, imaginative woman, but unfortunately delicate in constitution. "From his very birth his temper has been peculiar; pleasing, intelligent, and attaching, when his mind was undisturbed, and he was in the company of people who treated him reasonably and kindly; but exceedingly impatient under vexatious circumstances; very much disposed to find his own amusement in teasing and vexing others; and almost entirely incorrigible when it was necessary to reprove him. I never could find a successful mode of treating him. Harshness made him obstinate and gloomy; calm and long displeasure made him stupid and sullen; and kind patience had not sufficient power over his feelings to force him to govern himself. His disposition to worry made his appearance the perpetual signal for noise and disturbance among his brothers and sisters; and this it was impossible to stop, though a taste for quiet, and constant weak health, made it to me almost insupportable. After a statement of such great faults, it may seem an inconsistency to say, that he nevertheless still bore about him strong marks of a promising character. In all points of substantial principle his feelings were just and high. He had (for his age) an unusually deep feeling of admiration for everything that was good and noble; his relish was lively, and his taste good, for all the pleasures of the imagination; and he was also quite conscious of his own faults, and *(untempted)* had a just dislike to them. On these grounds I built my hopes that his reason would gradually correct his temper, and do that for him which his friends could not accomplish."

We shall see presently in what way his mother's hope was fulfilled, and how a naturally impatient and impetuous disposition was brought by strenuous self-discipline into captivity to the obedience of Christ's law.

In the meanwhile, as a young Fellow of Oriel, "his figure and manner were such as to command the confidence and affection of those about him. Tall, erect, very thin, never resting or sparing himself, investigating and explaining with unwearied energy, incisive in his language, and with a certain fiery force of look and tone, he seemed a sort of angelic presence to weaker natures. He slashed at the shams, phrases, and disguises in which the lazy or the pretentious veil their real ignorance or folly. His features readily expressed every varying mood of playfulness, sadness, and awe. There were those about him who would rather writhe under his most cutting sarcasms than miss their part in the workings of his sympathy and genius."

"Froude was a Tory, with that transcendental idea of the English gentleman which forms the basis of Toryism. He was a high Churchman of the uncompromising school, very early taking part with Anselm, Bechet, Laud, and the Nonjurors. Woe to anyone who dropped in his hearing such phrases as the dark ages, superstition, bigotry, right of private judgment, enlightenment, march of mind, or progress. When a stray man of science fell back on 'law,' or a 'subtle medium,' or any other device for making matter its own lord and master, it was as if a fox had broken cover; there ensued a chase and no mercy.

"Luxury, show, and even comfort he despised and denounced. He very consistently urged that the expenses of Eton should be kept down so low as to enable every ordinary incumbent to send his sons there to be trained for the ministry. All his ideas of college life were frugal and ascetic."

Dr. Newman speaks of Froude "as a man of high genius, brimful and overflowing with ideas and views, in him original, which were too many and strong for his bodily strength, and which crowded and jostled against each other in their effort after distinct shape and expression. And he had an intellect as critical and logical as it was speculative and bold. Dying prematurely, as he did, and in the conflict and transition-state of opinion, his religious views never reached their ultimate conclusion, by the very reason of their multitude and their depth."

It is possible, of course, as Dr. Newman would seem to imply, that Froude would have "gone over" side by side, or rather, in advance of his fellow leader, for Froude was one to be in advance generally of those with whom he journeyed. On the other hand we must give due weight to the fact that Froude, as Dr. Newman himself tells us, was an Englishman to the backbone in his severe adherence to the real and the concrete. Froude came back from Italy much more disgusted than Newman was with the practical abuses of Romanism, as exhibited in that country, where Romanism has freest play. He came home "even more utterly set against Roman Catholics than he had been before. His conclusion was that they held the truth in unrighteousness; that they were wretched Tridentines everywhere, and, of course, ever since the Reformation; that the conduct and behaviour of the clergy was such that it was impossible they could believe what they professed, that they were idolaters in the sense of substituing easy and good-natured divinities for the God of Truth and Holiness."

Before going abroad "he professed openly his admiration of the Church of Rome, and his hatred of the Reformers. He delighted in the notion of an hierarchical system, of sacerdotal power, and of full ecclesiastical liberty." ..... "He was smitten with the love of the Theocratic Church; he went abroad and was shocked by the degeneracy which he thought he saw in the Catholics of Italy." Dr. Newman goes on to say, a few lines lower down, "He taught me to look with admiration towards the Church of Rome, and in the same degree to dislike the Reformation. He fixed deep in me the idea of devotion to the Blessed Virgin, and he led me gradually to believe in the Real Presence."

There are other sides of his life, however, even more interesting and significant than those which we have considered.

His *Remains*, which were published in 1838 by Mr. Keble and Mr. Newman, came like a bombshell upon the religious world, vexed though it had been already, for some years, by the discussion of the questions raised by the Tractarian School. For the question thereby suggested to the vast majority of common-sense, respectable, English Christians was this:—Can Mr. Froude's life and tone of thought be what God demands of us? For one thing at least is certain— if Mr. Froude was right we are hopelessly wrong. There was no record here of the stereotyped experience of the eminent evangelical. A profane or careless youth followed by agonies of remorse; then an effulgence of gospel light in the soul, succeeded by a glorious career of self-satisfaction and popularity, the unstinted portion of the hero of a hundred muffin-worries.

Mr. Keble and Mr. Newman, who edited Hurrell Froude's *Remains* were rather intent on bringing before the world the picture of the inner life of a soul more intent upon the knowledge of itself and of its God, than careful for this world's censure or praise; and they were careful to express their own general coincidence in the opinions and feelings of their friend. The most daring publisher of diaries and private correspondence has never yet offered for sale the record of a self-analysis more thorough or minute. A few instances may serve to show the carefulness with which he sought to pierce to the innermost springs of motive and to sit in judgment upon his own lightest actions.

"Yesterday, when I went out shooting, I fancied I did not care whether I hit or not; but when it came to the point, I found myself anxious, and, after having killed, was not unwilling to let myself be considered a better shot than I described myself. I had an impulse, too, to let it be thought that I had only had three shots when I really had had four. It was slight, to be sure, but I felt it." . . . . . . "While I was thinking all this, I went into L—'s room to seek a pair of shoes, and on hearing him coming, got away as silently as possible. Why did I do this? Did I think I was doing what L— did not like? or was it the relic of a sneaking habit?" . . . . . "I was very hungry, but because I thought the charge unreasonable, I tried to shirk the waiter." . . . . . "I talked sillily to-day, as I used to do last term, but took no pleasure in it, so I am not ashamed." . . . . . "Looked with greediness to see if there was goose on the table for dinner." . . . . . "Tasted nothing till tea time, and then only one cup and dry bread." . . . . . "I have kept my fast strictly, having taken nothing till near nine this evening, and then only a cup of tea and a little bread without butter, but it has not been as easy as it was last." . . . . . "I made rather a more hearty tea than usual, quite giving up the notion of a fast in W—'s rooms, and by this weakness have occasioned another slip."

" Felt once as if I would have accepted ——'s invitation on Friday if I had expected a party to my taste ; and believe my motive was not sound at the bottom, as I am afraid is the case with all my motives. I read and go to chapel, because they are helps to get through the day. I use self-denial because I believe it the way to make the most of our pleasures ; and, besides, it has a tendency to give me what is essential to taking my place in society—self-command." . . . .

" Threw after I— his great-coat when he was on horseback, and when he was in a rage at my stupidity ; I felt like a fool, and affected to pass it off as a joke ; the consciousness of this folly, and the notion that I was seen through and despised for it, put me horribly out of sorts ; I have got right again, however, and am all comfortable." . . . .

. . . . " Meant to have kept a fast, and did abstain from dinner ; but at tea ate buttered toast, when I knew it was bad for me ; yet all the while was excusing myself, under the notion that I ought to prepare for the journey I should have to-day. I feel yet less as I get nearer to Oxford, and that I shall have to keep a sharp look-out on myself. I said my prayers inattentively yesterday and to-day. Have rather stuffed at breakfast —cannot help taking my money out at a meal—must get rid of this vulgar feeling."

" Was disgustingly ostentatious at dinner in asking for a china plate directly I had finished my meat. I did it on purpose, too, that the others might see I ate so much less than they did. Read affectedly in evening chapel." . . . " It crossed me I should like N— to observe that I had studied the service before I came to chapel, by my finding the lesson before it was given out." . . . " Felt an impulse of pleasure on finding W— was not at chapel this morning. I am always trying to persuade myself that I endeavour to be better than other people." . . . . " I think it was ostentatious in me to hint to S— that I got up at six o'clock." . . . .

" I sometimes try to assume a dignified face as I meet men, and am never content to be treated as a shilly-shally fellow." . . . " When W— said he did not dine in hall, I was conscious it would annoy me to think that he fasted. It proves that I do it that I may think myself good." . . . . " Instead of attending to the confession in morning chapel I was thinking whether any one had observed that I never missed this term." . . . . " Felt great reluctance to sleep on the floor last night, and was nearly arguing myself out of it; was not up till half-past six." . . . . " Felt ashamed that my trowsers were dirty whilst I was sitting next ——, but resolved not to hide them."

It may be granted at once that a spirit so self-observant as that of R. H. Froude could never have attained to any exceptional eminence as a man of affairs, or as a consoler of the sorrows of others; but on the other hand it may fairly be claimed for him that he stamped on the Tractarian movement in its earliest days the thought of the wonderful power of the ascetic life. There is no great danger of self-examination and fasting being practised with undue severity by the majority of English Churchmen, and a small collection of selections from the " Remains " might even now, if reprinted in a handy form, serve well to stimulate thought in the minds of the easy, the luxurious, and the self-satisfied.

It must be said, however, that the work in question

excited much justifiable objection by its bitter attacks upon many of the most highly-honoured Protestant names, and by its obviously strong leanings to the Church of Rome. We find Mr. Froude expressing himself thus: " Really, I hate the Reformation and the Reformers more and more, and have almost made up my mind that the rationalist spirit they set afloat is the ψευδοπροφήτης of the Revelations." . . . " Why do you praise Ridley ? Do you know sufficient good about him to counterbalance the fact that he was the associate of Cranmer, Peter Martyr and Bucer ? " . . . " I wish you could get to know something of S— and W—" (Southey and Wordsworth), " and un-Protestantise, un-Miltonise them." . . . " How is it we are so much in advance of our generation ?"

Again Mr. Froude visited the West Indies, and his sympathy with the Emancipation Movement can have been but slight if we are to judge by the following paragraphs :—

" I have felt it a kind of duty to maintain in my mind an habitual hostility to the niggers, and to chuckle over the failures of the new system, as if these poor wretches concentrated in themselves all the whiggery, dissent, cant, and abomination that have been ranged on their side."

. . . . . " Every one I meet seems to me like an incarnation of the whole Anti-Slavery Society, and Fowel Buxton at their head."

Again, his brother has told us how he used to speak of the Evangelical clergy as " fellows who turned up the whites of their eyes and said ' *Lawd.*' "

But, however narrow on some points Mr. R. H. Froude's views may have been, it is at least certain that to many of the ablest men of his party he appeared a singularly impressive person. His father, the Archdeacon, was a justice of the peace, and connected by family and fortune with the landed interest,—a man whose advice was much sought after, and known by his children as "a continually busy, useful man of the world, a learned and cultivated antiquary, and an accomplished artist." The spiritual lessons of his children did not go beyond the Catechism, and they were told that their business in life was to work and make for themselves an honourable position. He was too solid a man to be carried off his feet by the Oxford enthusiasm, but was a High Churchman of the old school. Still Mr. J. A. Froude tells us,—" The phrases and formulas of Anglo-Catholicism had become household words in our family before I understood coherently what the stir and tumult was about." The same writer described in the *Nemesis of Faith* an experience which we can hardly help regarding as most probably a personal recollection,—" Just as I was leaving off being a boy, we fell under a strong Catholicising influence at home, and I used to hear things that were strange enough to my ear. Faber was put away out of my studies; Newton was forbidden; and Davison, that I thought so dry and dull, put in his place. Transubstantiation was talked of before me as more than possible; celibacy of the clergy and fasting on the fast days were not only not wrong, but the very thing most needful . . . . our own dinners, indeed, did not suffer diminution . . . but even to raise the question was sufficiently alarming, and I sat by in silence, listening with the strangest sensations."

Mr. J. A. Froude has also in later years told us of his once well-known elder brother, who died ere he was himself eighteen,—" His course, whatever it was, would have been direct and straightforward; he was a man far more than a theologian; and if he had gone (to Rome), he would have gone with his whole heart and conscience, unassisted by subtleties and nice distinctions." ... " The terminus, however, towards which he and his friends were moving, had not come in sight in my brother's lifetime. He went forward, hesitating at nothing, taking the fences as they came, passing lightly over them all, and sweeping his friends along with him. He had the contempt of an intellectual aristocrat for private judgment and the rights of a man.... But he belonged, himself, to the class whose business was to order rather than obey. If his own bishop had interfered with him, his theory of episcopal authority would have been found inapplicable to that particular instance."

Keble, whose pupil Hurrell Froude at one time was, again and again speaks of him in his letters "in the most loving language, yet often not without some degree of anxiety as to his future course; he saw the elements of danger in him, how liable he might be to take the wrong course, or be misunderstood even when taking the right one; yet his hopes largely prevailed; and especially I remember his rejoicing at his being elected Fellow of Oriel, thinking that the new society and associations, with the responsibilities of college employment, would tend to keep him safe." Sir J. T. Coleridge, to whom we are indebted for the preceding paragraph, goes on to express his opinion that though Froude in the last years of his life may have come to more entire agreement with Newman as to action, yet there still remained a closer intimacy and more filial feeling on his part with regard to Keble.

John Henry Newman was born in London early in

1801. His father was of a family of small landed proprietors in Cambridgeshire, and had an hereditary taste for music, which he bequeathed to his eldest son. John Newman was first chief clerk, and then partner, in a London banking firm, which, however, succumbed, along with many others, in 1816, under the pressure caused by the contraction of the currency and the rapid fall of prices upon the return of peace after Waterloo. He subsequently took the Alton Brewery, in Hampshire, which, however, could not be made to answer, though he seems to have tried his best to ensure success.

John Henry was intended by his parents for one of the legal professions, and he actually kept some terms at Lincoln's Inn, but from his earliest days he was accustomed to revel in spiritual speculations. He has told us how—"I used to wish the Arabian tales were true: my imagination ran on unknown influences, on magical powers, and talismans. . . . . I thought life might be a dream, or I an angel, and all this world a deception, my fellow-angels, by a playful device, concealing themselves from me, and deceiving me with the semblance of a material world." His brother-in-law, Mr. Mozley, speaks of him as "thinking of nothing but the openings he saw here and there through the drift into the glory beyond, he accepted from early years every text, every expression, every figure, every emblem, and every thought thereby suggested, as a solemn and abiding reality which it was good to live in. It would hardly be too much to say that he knew the Bible by heart."

His mother had been a child of a well-known Huguenot family, long known in the City of London as engravers and paper manufacturers, and the teaching which he received at her knee was "that modified

Calvinism which retained the Assembly's Catechism as a text, but put into young hands Watts, Baxter, Scott, Romaine, Newton, Milner, indeed, any writer who seemed to believe and feel what he wrote about."

However, when he was fourteen he read with pleasure Paine's Tracts against the Old Testament, as well as Hume's Essays. He also recollects copying out some French verses, perhaps Voltaire's, in denial of the immortality of the soul, and saying to himself something like "How dreadful, but how plausible!" We, find however, that about this same period in his boyhood he was very superstitious, and used constantly to cross himself on going into the dark.

He has described how, in later years, his breath was almost taken away with surprise on finding in the first page of his first Latin verse-book, begun by him when barely ten years of age, a device which he had drawn, and which consisted of a solid cross upright, and next to it a rosary with a little cross attached. The incident was the more remarkable as he had not been influenced by any Romish associations.

At the age of fifteen he experienced the great change never to be forgotten, through which some souls are called to pass. "He expected to be 'converted;' in due time he was converted; and the day and hour of his conversion he has ever remembered, and, no doubt, observed." Dr. Newman himself ascribes this turning-point in his spiritual history to the sermons and conversations of the Rev. Walter Mayers, of Pembroke College, Oxford, and the books which he put into his hands, all of the School of Calvin. One of the first books which he read was a work of Romaine's, from which he gathered the doctrine of final perseverance, of which he says, " I received it at once, and believed that the inward conversion of which I was conscious (and of which I still am more certain than that I have hands and feet), would last into the next life, and that I was elected to eternal glory. I have no consciousness that this belief had any tendency whatever to lead me to be careless about pleasing God. I retained it till the age of twenty-one, when it gradually faded away; but I believe that it had some influence on my opinions, in the direction of those childish imaginations which I have already mentioned, viz., in isolating me from the objects which surrounded me, in confirming me in my mistrust of the reality of material phenomena, and making me rest in the thought of two, and two only, absolute and luminously self-evident beings, myself and my Creator."

At a very early age he had been sent to a preparatory school of 300 boys at Ealing, said to be the best in the country, and rose almost at a bound to the head of the school. In later years he was "sensible of having lost something in not being a public-school man. He regarded with admiration and a generous kind of envy the facile and elegant construing which a man of very ordinary talents would bring with him from the sixth form of any public school."

"He very early mastered music as a science, and attained such a proficiency on the violin that, had he not become a Doctor of the Church, he would have been a Paganini. At the age of twelve he composed an opera."

From Ealing he went straight to Trinity College, Oxford, where he associated almost exclusively with John William Bowden, during his undergraduate years.

He had begun to read, in the declining fortunes of his family, the call to a higher and more congenial profession than that of the bar, but the change in his expectations was in one respect attended with unfortunate consequences.

In order to save expense as much as possible, he hurried on his reading, and with quite inadequate preparation, presented himself for his degree examination at the earliest possible time, Michaelmas, 1820, when he was not yet nineteen, being thus two or three years younger than his fellow-candidates. "Various explanations are given of what occurred. It is said that Newman was very ill; that he had no sleep latterly, and had neglected even to take food. It is also added that the examiners were not the men to discover a genius under this disguise.

"Newman always maintained that he had been too discursive to make the proper preparation; that he had been properly examined; and that he alone was answerable for his failure. The result in those days turned on the *vivâ voce* examination, not on the paper work, as now. When the class lists came out Newman was found 'under the line,' as low as then he could be. The comparison with those to whom higher honours were accorded, and with the examiners themselves, is at least suggestive."

Was there so much, however, to be surprised at? George Eliot was one of the three or four English writers who alone have stood on John Henry Newman's level during the present century; and if she did not begin to make her mark till past the meridian of life, can we wonder at her great compeer failing in his first serious trial of intellectual strength when weighted with almost every possible disadvantage?

For three years after taking his B.A. degree, Newman resided at Oxford, enjoying the much-prized position of a scholar of Trinity and friendships with Isaac Williams and W. J. Copeland—friendships not to be measured by the ordinary standards of human relationship—until his election to a Fellowship at Oriel.

During his undergraduate years he seems to have turned for spiritual food chiefly to the writings of Thomas Scott, of Aston Sandford, having already been seriously impressed by Laws' *Serious Call*, after reading which he thenceforth held with a full inward assent and belief the doctrine of eternal punishment, as delivered by our Lord Himself. He had, moreover, at the age of fifteen, made acquaintance with two books which, each contrary to each, as he says, " planted in me the seeds of an intellectual inconsistency, which disabled me for a long course of years."

The one was Milner's Church History, in which he was enamoured of the long extracts from S. Augustine, S. Ambrose, and other Fathers, which seemed to him as the religion of the primitive Christians.

The other was Newton's work on the Prophecies, which stamped his mind with the notion that the Pope was the Antichrist predicted by Daniel, S. Paul, and S. John.

To quote Dr. Newman's own words, " My imagination was stained by the effects of this doctrine up to the year 1843; it had been obliterated from my reason and judgment at an earlier date; but the thought remained upon me as a sort of false conscience."

He goes on, a few lines further, in most interesting and touching words, to uplift the curtain from before yet another of the innermost recesses of his personal life, " I am obliged to mention, though I do it with great reluctance, another deep imagination, which at this time, the autumn of 1816, took possession of me; there can be no mistake about the fact, viz., that it would be the will of God that I should lead a single life. This anticipation, which has held its ground almost continuously ever since—with the break of a month now and a month then, up to 1829, and, after that break, without any break at all—was more or less connected in my mind with the notion that my calling in life would require such a sacrifice as celibacy involved; as, for instance, missionary work amongst the heathen, to which I had a great drawing for some years. It also strengthened my feeling of separation from the visible world, of which I have spoken above."

It was in 1823 that Newman was elected to a fellowship at Oriel, and most interesting would it be, if it were possible, to trace the opening out of his mind during the next two or three years, amid the society gathered there in that illustrious common room. A shy man, as he was, "with heart and mind in a continual ferment of emotion and speculation, yearning for sympathy and truth, was not likely to feel at home with some, whom it would be needless either to name or to describe. From the first he loved and admired the man with whom, eventually, he lived most in collision, Edward Hawkins."

He tells us himself how "During the first years of my residence at Oriel, though proud of my college, I was not quite at home there. I was very much alone, and I used often to take my daily walks by myself. I recollect once meeting Dr. Copleston, then Provost, with one of the fellows. He turned round, and with the kind courteousness which sat so well on him, made me a bow and said, *Nunquam minus solus, quàm cùm solus?* At that time, indeed (from 1823), I had the intimacy of my dear and true friend, Dr. Pusey, and could not fail to admire and revere a soul so devoted to the cause of religion, so full of good works, so faithful in his affections; but he left residence when I was getting to know him well. As to Dr. Whately himself, he was too much my superior to allow of my being at ease with him; and to no one in Oxford at this time did I open my heart fully and familiarly."

His intercourse with Whately might have been more satisfactory and lasting had Whately been content to demand from all his friends a less absolute submission to his own opinions. He was in many ways an admirable and most instructive master, but after a certain point his disciples were prone to fall away. He taught Newman, however, the existence of the Church as a substantive body or corporation, and made him an anti-Erastian.

In 1824 Newman took orders, and became Curate of S. Clement's, holding also the office of secretary of the local branch of the Church Missionary Society. In S. Clement's, had he not been accepted as an evangelical, he would never have been allowed to open his mouth; the Church, however, was soon filled, " and although his sermons, from the first, rather puzzled Mr. Hill and his weekly synod, they passed the censorship and were pronounced, on the whole, spiritual."

In 1825 Whately became Principal of S. Alban Hall, and Newman was as yet on such terms with him as to allow of his sharing as Vice-Principal in such tuition as could be given to the dozen young men there who only wanted to get a degree with a minimun expenditure of work.

Early in 1826 Newman became tutor of Oriel, and at Easter in the same year two Oriel bachelors were elected to fellowships at the same college—Robert Isaac Wilberforce and Richard Hurrell Froude. The former of these was second son of William Wilberforce, then member for Yorkshire, and leader in the Commons of the Emancipation movement. To the latter we have already given a few pages. With both of them Newman lived for many years on terms of particular intimacy and affection.

Newman's position as tutor now began to give him weight, and he had written one or two essays which had been well received. He preached his first university sermon. In 1827 he was one of the public examiners for the B.A. degree. In 1828 he became Vicar of S. Mary's. He says, speaking of this period, "It was to me like the feeling of spring weather after winter; and, if I may so speak, I came out of my shell; I remained out of it till 1841." ... "From this time my tongue was, as it were, loosened, and I spoke spontaneously and without effort."

One of his friends, a Mr. Rickards, said of him, "Here is a fellow who, when he is silent, will never begin to speak; and when he once begins to speak, will never stop." At this time he began to exert an influence over younger men, which steadily increased for a course of years.

In 1826 Newman published an essay on "Miracles," in which he considered that miracles were sharply divisible into two classes, those which were to be received, and those which were to be rejected; whereas, when he came to treat of the same subject some sixteen years later he saw that they were to be estimated according to their greater or less probability. In 1827 *The Christian Year* made its appearance, and the two main intellectual truths which it brought home to Newman were two which he had already learned from Butler's *Analogy*, though recast in Keble's creative mind. The first was what may be called the Sacramental System; that is, the doctrine that material phenomena are both the types and instruments of unseen realities. The second was the doctrine of probability, announced by Butler in all its dreary uncertain barrenness—an Upas tree under which truth withers down into a mere set of opinions—a doctrine, however, which Keble vivified by the admixture of Love and Faith, "which give to probability a force which it has not in itself. Faith and love are directed towards an object; in the vision of that object they live; it is that object, received by faith and love, which renders it reasonable to take probability as sufficient for internal conviction. Thus the argument from probability, in the matter of religion, became an argument from personality, which, in fact, is one form of the argument from authority." It may appear to less acute minds that Keble was easily satisfied in this case, and that he *assumed* the existence of an object, and then applying faith and love to that object, used them as proofs of the same object whose existence they had already assumed.

Newman says, "I did not at all dispute this view of the matter, for I made use of it myself; but I was dissatisfied, because it did not go to the root of the difficulty. It was beautiful and religious, but it did not even profess to be logical."

Newman, in his subsequent writings, tried to complete Keble's argument by considerations of his own, which may be fairly summarised by the statement that we are "bound to be more or less sure, on a sort of (as it were) graduated scale of assent, viz., according as the probabilities attaching to a professed fact were brought home to us."

In proportion as Newman moved out of the shadow

of that liberalism which Whately and his school had flung over the early years of his Oriel life, his early devotion towards the Fathers returned; and in the long vacation of 1828 he set about to read them chronologically, beginning with Ignatius and Justin.

In 1830, the year in which he found himself more at leisure, through his resignation of the duties of the tutorship, a proposal was made to him by Mr. Hugh James Rose and Mr. Lyall, to furnish them with a history of the principal councils, as a contribution to a theological library which they were endeavouring to bring out. Newman began with the Council of Nicœa, to find himself launched on the ocean of Church History with its currents innumerable. And his work at last appeared under the title of "The Arians of the Fourth Century."

While this work was in progress events of grave import were happening, both at home and on the Continent. Shortly before this time there had been a revolution in France, while in England the great Reform agitation was seething dangerously. The prelates of the Church had been insulted and threatened in the streets of London. There are a few still living who recollect "the fierce shout of applause which rent the air at a large public meeting at Canterbury when one of the speakers suggested that the noble cathedral of that city should be converted into a stable for the horses of the cavalry." Writing in January, 1831, Samuel Wilberforce says:—" When I look around with these feelings I see on every side the visible threatenings of Providence; a discontented people, one class pressing upon another, and all at war between themselves; an assaulted Church ill-defended; poor-laws making all paupers in order to provide an inheritance for the idle and the profligate; a demi-Radical government with the true march-of-mind spirit; and the whole of Europe shaken to its base by the volcanic throes of revolution; while such spirits as Cobbett, Hume, W. Harvey & Co., seem like insects before thunder, or sea-mews before a storm, instinctively to rejoice in the coming tempest."

There was every justification for this description of the times. In the autumn of the same year the sacking and burning of the Bishop's palace at Bristol—where Charles Kingsley, then a young boy, "seemed to be looking down upon Dante's Inferno, and to hear the multitudinous moan and wail of the lost spirits surging to-and-fro amid that sea of fire"—was only a most signal example of a feeling which pervaded the whole country.

"Even Archbishop Howley, on coming to Canterbury for his primary visitation, was insulted, spat upon, and only brought with difficulty by a circuitous route to the Deanery, amid the execrations of a furious mob. On the 5th of November, in many of the towns, and especially in the cathedral towns, the Bishops were substituted for Guy Fawkes, and the Bishops of Exeter and Winchester were burnt in effigy close to their own palace gates."

As we have already seen, the wildest schemes of concession and reform were being ventilated in the hope of saving the Church, ere all should be lost. The vital question to Newman and his circle of immediate friends was how to keep the Church from being Liberalised.

Speaking of this period and of his "History of the Arians," he writes—"With the Establishment thus divided and threatened, thus ignorant of its true strength, I compared that fresh vigorous Power of which I was reading in the first centuries. In her triumphant zeal on behalf of that Primeval Mystery, to which I had had so great a devotion from my youth, I recognised the movement of my Spiritual Mother. 'Incessu patuit Dea.' The self-conquest of her Ascetics, the patience of her Martyrs, the irresistible determination of her Bishops, the joyous swing of her advance, both exalted and abashed me. I said to myself, 'Look on this picture and on that;' I felt affection for my own Church, but not tenderness; I felt dismay at her prospects, anger and scorn at her do-nothing perplexity."

The "History of the Arians" was ready for the press in July, 1832, though not published till the end of 1833. The winter of those two years was spent by Newman in the south of Europe, most of the time in company with his friend Hurrell Froude, who had been ordered to winter abroad, to escape, if possible, the consumption which threatened him.

Newman would seem to have had little intercourse when abroad with foreign ecclesiastics, and to have had ample opportunities of noting the seamy side of Catholicism. He saw nothing, however, but what was external —of the hidden, devotional lives of the best Romanists he knew nothing. The enforced isolation of a stranger in a strange land drove him back upon himself, and the state of affairs in England was ever in his thoughts. Disgusted at the Liberal line which Blomfield, the Bishop of London, was taking, Newman sent home a refusal of one of the Whitehall preacherships, which had lately been put on a new footing, and which were filled by the most brilliant and rising teachers, both from Oxford and Cambridge.

In Sicily, Newman was struck down with a dangerous fever, which delayed his return home for many weeks. He was thought to be dying, but did not himself share in that opinion—his mind being all occupied with the belief that he had a work to do in England.

These months of travel were in fact a lull in the midst of the activities of a busy life, and a presentiment was gathering strength within him of a great coming destiny, now close at hand.

It now remains to indicate briefly some of the marvellous personal influence which Newman exercised over so many of his fellow-students at Oxford during the next twelve years—which made him the centre and head of the new school, of whom Mr. Mozley has observed,—" I may honestly say that, with the exception of Keble, I do not think one of them would be a living name a century hence, but for his share in the light of Newman's genius and goodness," and of whom Mr. J. A. Froude has written,—" Compared with him, they were all but as cyphers, and he the indicating number." The last-mentioned writer has given us a few touches of interesting personal description of the great teacher, whom he places side by side with Thomas Carlyle as the two writers who have affected most powerfully the present generation of Englishmen,— " His appearance was striking. He was above the middle height, slight and spare. His head was large, his face remarkably like that of Julius Cæsar. The forehead, the shape of the ears and nose, were almost the same. The lines of the mouth were very peculiar, and I should say exactly the same. I have often thought of the resemblance, and believed that it extended to the temperament. In both there was an original force of character, which refused to be moulded by circumstances, which was to make its own way, and become a power in the world; a clearness of intellectual perception, a disdain for conventionalities, a temper imperious and wilful, but along with it a most attaching gentleness, sweetness, singleness of heart and purpose. Both were formed by nature to command others, both had the faculty of attracting to themselves the passionate devotion of their friends and followers, and in both cases, too, perhaps the devotion was rather due to the personal ascendancy of the leader than to the cause which he represented. It was Cæsar, not the principle of the empire, which overthrew Pompey and the constitution. *Credo in Newmannum* was a common phrase at Oxford, and is still unconsciously the faith of nine-tenths of the English converts to Rome."

In these words, Mr. Froude, after the lapse of many years, described the influence of the man who had cast such a strange spell over his own early life. The same writer, shortly after parting company with the Tractarian party, published *The Nemesis of Faith*,—a work now almost lost sight of—in which one of the characters describes a substantially similar experience, the central figure to whom he alludes being sufficiently obvious,—" Well, as we had none of us any very clear idea to magnetise us, and as yet had not approached the point when the other influences would come to bear upon us, and we should begin to feel the gravitation downwards in the necessity of getting on in the world, the leader of the movement took us all his own way; all, that is, who were not Arnoldised. And even some of them he contrived to draw away by the nearness and continuance of his action upon them, as the comet's attraction played the deuce with Jupiter's satellites while it continued in their neighbourhood. It is true we thought, yes, we thought we were following the Church; but it was like the goose in the child's toy, which is led by the nose up and down the basin by the piece of bread .... by the piece of bread .... with the loadstone inside it," and again in another place,—"while, in fact, we were only Newmanites, we fancied we were becoming Catholics."

It would be a mistake, however, to suppose that Newman owed his influence to the potency of a majestic presence, as the term would be generally understood, or to the pomp and circumstances of a dignified and a lofty position. It was no ponderous Head of a House, announcing Catholic platitudes *ore rotundo*, who drew for many years such a heterogeneous crowd, the old and young, the diligent, the idle, the gifted and the dull, the pure and the vicious, round the pulpit of S. Mary's. It was only those who knew the inner as well as the outer man who realized his greatness. "Newman did not carry his head aloft or make the best use of his height. He did not stoop, but he had a slight bend forward, owing, perhaps, to the rapidity of his movements, and to his always talking while he was walking. His gait was that of a man upon serious business bent, and not on a promenade." He was impressive as appearing to live not so much here, as rather in the world unseen, and to be following truth, lead him were she might.

Mr. Mozley tells us: "There was no pride in his port or defiance in his eye. Though it was impossible to see him without interest, and, something more, he disappointed those who had known him only by name. They who saw for the first time the man whom some warm admirer had described in terms above common eulogy, found him so little like the great Oxford don or future pillar of the Church, that they said he might pass for a Wesleyan minister. John Wesley must have been a much more imposing figure. Robust and ruddy sons of the Church looked on him with condescending pity as a poor fellow whose excessive sympathy, restless energy, and general unfitness for this practical world, would soon wreck him. Thin, pale, and with large lustrous eyes ever piercing through this veil of men and things, he hardly seemed made for this world." . . . " His dress—it became almost the badge of his followers —was the long-tailed coat, not always very new." . . . " Newman, however, never studied his ' get-up,' or even thought of it. He had other uses for his income, which in these days would have been thought poverty."

"It became the fashion of the party to despise solemnity of manner and stateliness of gait. Newman walked quickly, and, with a congenial companion, talked incessantly." . . . " Yet he was never so busy or so preoccupied but that he had always upon him a burden of conscientious duties to be attended to, calls of civility or kindness, promises to be fulfilled, bits of thoughtfulness carried out, rules of his own to be attended to." Those, and they were many, who stood silent and entranced before the Cardinal's portrait in the great exhibition of this year at Manchester, and noted the square, perpendicular forehead, the quiet, yet all-scrutinising eye, the firmly-moulded jaw, and the refinement, tenderness and sweetness of the mouth, will hardly wonder at his having been so impressive sixty years ago in the eyes of those best qualified to judge.

"In Oriel Lane," writes the late Professor of Poetry at Oxford, Principal Shairp, "light-hearted undergraduates would drop their voices and whisper, 'there's Newman!' when, head thrust forward, and gaze fixed as though on some vision seen only by himself, with swift, noiseless step he glided by. Awe fell on them for a moment as if it had been some apparition that had passed."

Another Oxford Professor of Poetry, Mr. Matthew Arnold, writes in a like strain: "Who could resist the charm of that spiritual apparition, gliding in the dim afternoon light through the aisles of S. Mary's, rising into the pulpit, and then in the most entrancing of voices, breaking the silence with words and thoughts which were a religious music—subtle, sweet, mournful? I seem to hear him still, saying: 'After the fever of life, after wearinesses and sicknesses, fightings and despondings, languor and fretfulness, struggling and succeeding; after all the changes and chances of this troubled, unhealthy state—at length comes death, at length the white throne of God, at length the beatific vision.'"

It was noted by the author of *The Nemesis of Faith*, that while the talk of young University men about the outside world is, owing to their ignorance of that world, so unreal, their own selves, their risings, fallings, aspirings, resolutions, and misgivings are most real to them, and he goes on to observe: "It was into these that N—'s power of insight was so remarkable. I believe no young man ever heard him preach without fancying that some one had been betraying his own history, and the sermon was aimed specially at him. It was likely that, while he had possession so complete of what we did know about ourselves, we should take his word for what we did not; and while he could explain *us*, let him explain the rest for us." The same author writing many years later of the "Oxford Counter Reformation" tells us that, "Newman, taking some Scripture character for a text, spoke to us about ourselves, our temptations, our experiences. His illustrations were inexhaustible. He seemed to be addressing the most secret consciousness of each of us—as the eyes of a portrait appear to look at every person in a room. He never exaggerated; he was never unreal." On one occasion he tells us how "Newman described closely some of the incidents of our Lord's passion; he then paused. For a few moments there was a breathless silence. Then in a low, clear voice, of which the faintest vibration was audible in the farthest corner of S. Mary's, he said, 'Now, I bid you recollect that He to whom these things were done was Almighty God.' It was as if an electric shock had gone through the church, as if every person present understood for the first time the meaning of what he had all his life been saying."

Newman, however, was no mere theologian—"*Homo sum humani nihil a me alienum puto,*" might truthfully have fallen from his lips. He was wont to speak to his pupils and disciples of the ordinary subjects of the day— literature, public persons, and incidents—of anything in fact that was generally interesting, seeming always to know more about everything than anybody else. " He was never condescending with us, never didactic or authoritative; but what he said carried conviction along with it. When we were wrong he knew why we were wrong, and excused our mistakes to ourselves while he set us right." Remembering, then, that young Oxford numbered in those days some twelve hundred students, gathered from every quarter of the kingdom, and that they returned to their homes thrice a year—and that no inconsiderable portion of them went back, their mouths full of what Newman had been saying—can we wonder that his name became one of very considerable magnitude, curiosity, and suspicion in the religious world of that day.

CHAPTER IV.

THE "HOW"—THE TRACTS FOR THE TIMES.

WE have seen how Mr. Newman returned to England from the south of Europe in the early summer of 1833, a few days before Mr. Keble preached the Assize Sermon in the Oxford University Pulpit, which was shortly afterwards published under the title of *National Apostacy*, and which Mr. Newman has ever since regarded as the start of that great upheaval in the English Church, often known under the name of the Tractarian Movement. The text of that sermon had been "The noble declaration of Samuel as to the course which he will continue to pursue in regard to his countrymen, when they insisted on renouncing their Theocracy, and on being governed by a king as the Gentiles were."

At the time when this sermon was preached, the measures then in progress in regard to the Established Church of Ireland, which ended, before its publication, in the suppression of the bishoprics, weighed heavily on Mr. Keble's mind.

Mr. Newman has told us how, on getting home from abroad, he found that a movement had already commenced in opposition to the specific danger which seemed to be threatening the religion of the nation and its church. "Several zealous and able men had united their counsels, and were in correspondence with each other. The principal of these were Mr. Keble, Hurrell Froude, who had reached home long before me, Mr. William Palmer of Dublin and Worcester College (not Mr. William Palmer of Magdalen, who is now a Catholic), Mr. Arthur Perceval, and Mr. Hugh Rose."

The last named of this little company is the only one deserving of special notice. Mr. E. B. Birks has stated quite recently :—"*Apropos* of the origin of the Oxford Movement, the late Master of Trinity, Cambridge, remarked to me one day that Hugh James Rose, a Cambridge man, was the true founder of it."

Without going so far as that, we may safely say that in the earliest days of the movement, Mr. Rose was one of the most, probably the most valuable, of its supporters outside Oxford. We cannot do better than listen to Mr. Newman's account of his eminent fellow-labourer :—" To mention Mr. Hugh Rose's name is to kindle in the minds of those who knew him, a host of pleasant and affectionate remembrances. He was the man above all others fitted by his cast of mind and literary powers to make a stand, if a stand could be made, against the calamity of the times. He was gifted with a high and large mind, and a true sensibility of what was great and beautiful ; he wrote with warmth and energy ; and he had a cool head and cautious judgment" .... " In order under such grave circumstances to unite churchmen together, and to make a front against the coming danger, he had, in 1832 commenced the *British Magazine* ; and in the same year he came to Oxford in the summer term, in order to beat up for writers for his publication ; on that occasion I became known to him through Mr. Palmer. His reputation and position came in aid of his obvious fitness, in point of character and intellect, to become the centre of an ecclesiastical movement, if such a movement were to depend on the action of a party. His delicate health, his premature death, would have frustrated the expectation even though the new school of opinion had been more exactly thrown into the shape of a party, than in fact was the case. But he zealously backed up the first efforts of those who were principals in it; and, when he went abroad to die, in 1838, he allowed me the solace of expressing my feelings of attachment and gratitude to him by addressing him in the dedication of a volume of my sermons as the man ' who, when hearts were failing, bade us stir up the gift that was in us, and betake ourselves to our true mother.' "

Within a very few days of Newman's return home he was in communication with Rose, and after much correspondence a meeting of kindred spirits took place at Hadleigh in Suffolk, of which parish Rose was rector. To quote from Mr. Mozley—" They were rallying round the Church of England, its Prayer Book, its faith, its ordinances, its constitution, its Catholic and Apostolic Character; all more or less assailed by foes and in abeyance even with friends. The suppression of Irish sees gave immediate prominence to the doctrine of Apostolic succession, which it was said to set at nought."

The author of the *Nemesis of Faith* has thrown a lurid light upon the times as they must have seemed to the little band of reformers, and his description serves to explain several expressions used by Mr. Newman in the passages which we have just quoted:—" What a sight must this age of ours have been to an earnest believing man like Newman, who had an eye to see it, and an ear to hear its voices? A foolish Church, chattering parrot-like old notes, of which it had forgotten the meaning; a clergy who not only thought not at all, but whose heavy ignorance, from long unreality, clung about them like a garment, and who mistook their fool's cap and bells for a crown of wisdom, and the music of the spheres;

selfishness alike recognized practically as the rule of conduct, and faith in God, in man, in virtue, exchanged for faith in the belly, in fortunes, carriages, lazy sofas, and cushioned pews; Bentham politics, and Paley religion; all the thought deserving to be called thought, the flowing tide of Germany, and the philosophy of Hume and Gibbon; all the spiritual feeling, the light froth of the Wesleyans and Evangelicals; and the only real stern life to be found anywhere, in a strong resolved and haughty democratic independence, heaving and rolling underneath the chaff-spread surface. How was it like to fare with the clergy gentlemen, and the Church turned respectable, in the struggle with enemies like these? Erastianism, pluralities, prebendal stalls, and pony-gigging parsons,—what work were they like to make against the proud, rugged, intellectual republicanism, with a fire-sword between its lips, bidding cant and lies be still; and philosophy, with Niebuhr criticism for a reaping sickle, mowing down their darling story-books? High time it was to move indeed. High time for the Church warriors to look about them, to burnish up their armour, to seize what ground was yet remaining, what time to train for the battle. It would not serve to cultivate the intellect. All over Europe, since Spinoza wrote, what of strongest intellect there was had gone over to the enemy. Genius was choosing its own way, acknowledging no longer the authority either of man or document; and unless in some way or other the heart could be pre-occupied—unless the Church could win back the love of her children, and temper them quite differently from the tone in which they were now tempered, the cause was lost—and for ever. So, then, they must begin with the clergy. To wean the Church from its Erastianism into militancy, where it might at least command respect for its sincerity—to wean the bishops from their palaces and lazy carriages and fashionable families, the clergy from their snug firesides and marrying and giving in marriage: this was the first step. Slowly then to draw the people out the whirl of business to thought upon themselves—from self-assertion; from the clamouring for their rights, and the craving for independence, to almsgiving, to endurance of wrong, to the confessional—from doing to praying—from early hours in the office, or in the field, to matins and daily service: this was the purpose of the Tract movement."

Such is Mr. Froude's summary of the causes which led to the Hadleigh Conference, and of the aim which those who attended it had in view; nor can we deny that he has stated the case with substantial accuracy and fairness.

To quote, then, again from Mr. Mozley, " In two or three weeks accordingly appeared that portentous birth of time, the *Tracts for the Times*. Tracts had long been the most familiar form of religious propagandism, and there were many thousands of ladies and gentlemen who made it their business to deliver tracts by the house row, by the post, or to anybody they chanced to meet. Yet this was a startling novelty. The distributors of tracts, that is, the clergy and educated classes, had hitherto enjoyed themselves an exemption from tracts. So this was to turn their own battery against them. There were, too, great practical difficulties. The booksellers did not like tracts. They are litter; they occupy space; they encumber accounts; they don't pay. Messrs. Rivington, however, undertook the London publication, it must be presumed for conscience sake. For the convenience of the publishers they were to come out with the monthlies. They were to be anonymous and by different hands, each writer singly responsible." In regard to Messrs. Rivington's connection with the publication, we must note the following entry in Mr. Pattison's diary: "Newman thinks Rivington very well disposed; took up the Oxford Tracts just about the time that the P.C.K. Society was taken from him."

The *Tracts for the Times*, of which a complete list will be found at the end of this chapter, were published at intervals during the years which followed 1833, until they were brought to an abrupt conclusion in 1841. The first seventy followed each other in quick succession, were of slight extent, and were sold at a penny or twopence apiece. The last twenty appeared at longer intervals, were more ample in the treatment of their subjects, and for the most part ranged in price from sixpence up to a shilling.

The advertisement to Volume I., which includes Tracts 1 to 46, begins as follows:—" The following Tracts were published with the object of contributing something towards the practical revival of doctrines which, although held by the great divines of our Church, at present have become obsolete with the majority of her members, and are withdrawn from public view even by the more learned and orthodox few who still adhere to them. The Apostolic Succession, the Holy Catholic Church, were principles of action, in the minds of our predecessors of the seventeenth century; but in proportion as the maintenance of the Church has been secured by law, her ministers have been under the temptation of leaning on an arm of flesh instead of her own divinely-provided discipline, a temptation increased by political events and arrangements, which need not here be more than alluded to."

The advertisement goes on to point out how, owing to the forgetfulness and neglect of her true powers and teaching on the part of the Church, methodism and popery were in different ways the refuges of souls destitute of a proper supply of those means of grace which they should have been able to enjoy in their fulness within her walls.

As was but natural, however, the religious world was but slowly moved, and the Tracts were for some two or three years as seed cast on the waters. The advertisement to Volume II., dated The Feast of All Saints, 1835, reports progress in the following terms:—" In completing the second volume of a publication, to which the circumstances of the day have given rise, it may be right to allude to a change which has taken place in them since the date of its commencement. At that time, in consequence of long security, the attention of members of our Church had been but partially engaged in ascertaining the grounds of their adherence to it; but the imminent peril to which all that is dear to them has since been exposed, has naturally turned their thoughts that way, and obliged them to defend it on one or other of the principles which are usually put forward on its behalf. Discussions have thus been renewed in various quarters, on points which had long remained undisturbed; and, though numbers continue undecided in opinion, or take up a temporary position in some one of the hundred middle points which may be assumed between the two main theories in which the question issues, and others, again, have deliberately entrenched themselves in the modern or ultra-protestant alternative, yet, on the whole, there has been much hearty and intelligent adoption, and much respectful study, of those more primitive views maintained by our great divines."

The same advertisement goes on, however, to admit that the acceptance of the principles propounded in the Tracts thus far issued, was in many cases far from deeply-rooted, or practically effective ; and that much more had been done " in awakening Churchmen to the truth of the Apostolic Commission as a fact, and to the admission of it as a duty, than to the enjoyment of it as a privilege."

The advertisement to Volume III., dated a year later, viz., Feast of All Saints, 1836, in speaking of the substitution, as time went on, of Tracts of considerable extent for the short and incomplete papers with which the publication commenced, defends the earlier tracts as having been "written with the hope of rousing members of our Church to comprehend her alarming position, of helping them to realize the fact of the gradual growth, allowance, and establishment of unsound principles in the management of her internal concerns ; and having this object they spontaneously used the language of alarm and complaint. They were written as a man might give notice of a fire or inundation, to startle all who heard him, with only so much of doctrine and argument as might be necessary to account for their publication or might answer more obvious objections to the views therein advocated."

There was not indeed entire unanimity among the leaders of the movement in regard to the issue of the tracts.

Mr. Palmer from the first objected to them, and in consequence withdrew from the Association and held aloof. He represented to some extent the orthodox high and dry Church dignitaries, who were then, as always, opposed to the irresponsible action of individuals, and whose *beau ideal* is certain to be a board of safe, sound, and sensible men. Mr. Hurrell Froude's absence from England and his premature death, and the withdrawal of Mr. Palmer, had the effect of leaving the responsibility of the publication almost entirely in the hands of Mr. Newman and Mr. Keble, who were joined in the later part of 1833 by Dr. Pusey, who was at once recognized as a tower of strength to the cause.

Mr. Newman in replying to the remonstrances of Mr. Palmer and Mr. Percival wrote as follows :—" As to the Tracts, every one has his own taste. You object to some things, another to others. If we altered to please every one, the effect would be spoiled. They were not intended as symbols *è cathedrâ*, but as the expression of individual minds; and individuals, feeling strongly, while on the one hand, they are incidentally faulty in mode or language, are still peculiarly effective. No great work was done by a system; whereas systems rise out of individual exertions. Luther was an individual. The very faults of an individual excite attention; he loses, but his cause (if good and he powerful minded) gains. This is the way of things; we promote truth by a self-sacrifice."

The Tracts were advertised as written by members of the University of Oxford, but the particular writers were soon known, were indeed proud to be known, and thus practically became personally responsible.

Pre-eminent amongst the writers was of course Mr. Newman. The other contributors " wrote sermons or treatises, but not tracts. They discharged the contents of their commonplace books, or they compiled from indexes, and thought it impossible to give too much of a good thing. Compared with Newman's, their tracts were stuffing and make-weights, learned, wise, and good, but not calculated to take hearts by storm."

And now in regard to the methods employed to push the circulation of the tracts. Mr. Newman has mentioned a series of experiments which he made in this direction in the course of the year 1833. He called upon many of the clergy in many parts of the country, whether he was acquainted with them or not, and attended gatherings of the clergy held at the houses of his own friends. Many of his friends were active in the same work. Mr. Mozley tells us how :—" The tracts had to be circulated by post, by hand, or anyhow, and many a young clergyman spent days in riding about with a pocketful, surprising his neighbours at breakfast, lunch, dinner, and tea. The correspondence that ensued was immense. Nobody was too humble in intellect or in clerical position not to be invited, and enrolled as an ally. Men survive, or have but lately passed away, who can never have known what it was to share a glory and a greatness except at that happy time. The world would now wonder to see a list of the great Cardinal's friends. He had a remarkable quality which presents a strange contrast to the common habit of vulgar depreciators. Like Walter Scott, he could only see the best and highest parts of the human character, hoping ever against hope. He expected rivers out of the dry ground, and found poetic beauty in the quaintest and most rugged writers. Wise and experienced Oxford observers smiled at the confidence he reposed in men who were at best broken reeds and bulrushes, if not stocks and stones. He could appreciate writers whom nobody else could, seeing sense in their obscurity and life in their dullness."

Much to the same effect, writing of the state of the movement a few years later, Mr. Pattison observes :— " Indeed, it was a general wonder how Newman himself could be content with the society of men like Bowles, Coffin, Dalgairus, St. John, Lockhart, and others."

And now, in order to estimate aright the general influence of the *Tracts* upon the Church for good or evil, we may as well call into court a few witnesses of various schools of thought. We will begin with Sir J. T. Coleridge, author of *Keble's Memoir*, who writes as follows : " It is, in my opinion, mere prejudice to deny that the cause of true religion, and of the Church of England, reaped great advantage from the circulation of the *Tracts ;* one must have been a quiet and attentive observer of the state of the parochial clergy, and of the English Church generally before they were issued, to be a competent judge of this. Making every allowance for exaggeration, the change for the better is great, and to be observed not so much in bright instances here and there, as in the general tone of feeling and conduct, in the higher appreciation of what the profession requires of its members, and the larger and more distinct acknowledgment of duty. In these respects I think it may be said, comparing the two periods, that the rule has become the exception, the exception the rule. But it will be equally prejudice, as it seems to me, to deny that incidentally some evil flowed from them. I remember on occasion of some early secessions to Rome it was reported to have been said by Dr. Pusey, that however much he regretted it, he could not deny that some were to be anticipated,—it was a sensible remark, if I may be allowed to say so. The Tracts came at a time when we were (speaking of the generality both lay and clerical) wholly untrained in dogmatic theology, wholly unversed in the questions which lay between the Roman and the English branches of Christ's Church.

"Elderly men will remember the time when, for students to go into the controversy with Rome was thought nearly superfluous, and for clergymen to preach on it a mere waste of time. The *Tracts* stirred this tranquil, perhaps stagnant, lake; and the stir of men's minds, especially among the younger and more ardent, naturally produced enquiry, under circumstances not at all favourable to a just result; the imperfect practice, and the theory in some instances not strictly logical or complete of our Church, were arraigned without that diffident reverence, or that due allowance for circumstances, which might have been reasonably expected; and there was the crowning fallacy 'if not England, then Rome;' on behalf of which latter every assumption was made."

Let us turn now to the verdict of Dr. Hook, who was recognized by the Tractarian leaders as the ablest exponent of the practical working out of their views in a large town parish. In a note to a sermon preached in 1838, he observes: "The reputed writers of the *Tracts* were men of ardent piety, who had been attached to the Evangelical school, and it was among the younger men who had been educated in that school that they created a strong sensation. Hence, perhaps, the bitterness with which they are assailed by some of the older partizans of that section of the Church. To those who, like the present writer, had been educated strictly on the principles of the English Reformation, and belonged to the old orthodox school, they brought forward nothing new; and though we may have demurred to some of their opinions, and have thought that in some things they were in an extreme, we rejoice to see right principles advocated in a manner so decided, and in a spirit so truly Christian. . . . . I am not one of those who would say, 'Read the Oxford *Tracts*, and take for granted every opinion there expressed;' but I am one of those who would say, 'Read and digest these *Tracts* well, and you will have imbibed principles which will enable you to judge of opinions.' Their popularity will increase, since their arguments are not answered or their statements confuted: they are opposed simply by railing. And those who judge of such things only by second-hand reports and garbled quotations, and anonymous misrepresentations in newspapers, will, of course, rail on. May the day come when they may be awakened to a sense of the danger of thus violating the golden rule of charity. In the meantime the wise, the candid, those who are not the mere partizans of religion, but really religious, will themselves read the *Tracts;* and if they do read they will commend. They may censure particular opinions, but they will commend the whole."

There are, of course, frequent references to the *Tracts* in the *Life of Bishop Wilberforce*, one or two of which possess a certain interest. On Good Friday, 1835, the following entry occurs:—" Read Pusey's tractate on fasting—am convinced by it, if not of the duty, yet certainly of the expediency of conforming to the rules of the Church on this point. I think it likely to be especially useful to me in three ways: first in enabling me to *realize* unseen things; one of my special difficulties. Second, as likely to help me in prayer, in which I am greatly interrupted by an unbridled indolence. Third, in helping me to subdue the body to the spirit, which I think very needful for me."

Again, writing to Mr. Chas. Anderson on May 31, 1836, he says:—" Do you see the *Tracts for the Times?* they are very well worth your reading. There are two octavo volumes now published of them, which I wish you would get and read. It is the view of Baptism which seems to me to be pushed too far. I mean the deadly state to which they picture sin after baptism to reduce men."

Once more, writing to the same friend in 1838, Wilberforce observes:—" I agree with all *you say* about the Oxford School; but *I have some fears.* When did the minds of men not run into extremes? My principal fears are, that they will lead to the depression of true individual spirituality of mind in the reaction of their minds, from the *self-idolizing tendency* of the late leading religious party, by leading others to elevate solely the *systematic* and communion part of Christianity; that they will disgust some well-intentioned Churchmen by a fanciful imitation of antiquity, and drive them into lower depths of 'Peculiarity.' I cannot use all their language about the Eucharist; I cannot bear Pusey's new sin after baptism. They hold up a glorious standard of holiness, and for *us*, my dear Charles, who know well the hope of the Gospel, and can supply all they leave deficient, it is the very thing needful, but there are ignorant and bowed-down souls who need a more welcoming treatment than their views of penitence will allow."

Perhaps, however, Mr. Wilberforce hit the Tractarian writers his hardest blow when he spoke of them to Dr. Hook as "enforcing an ancient practice at the expense of a still more ancient principle."

In the letters of the late Charles Kingsley, a man of keen and vigorous intellect, there are frequent allusions to the writings of the Tractarian School. The subjoined samples will enable us to estimate his attitude toward them.

May 10th, 1842.—"We must be Catholic; we must hold the whole truth; we must have no partial or favourite views of Christianity, like the Dissenters and the Tractarians. The more I look, the more I see how superior the divines of the seventeenth century were to the present generation, and how they have been belied by the Tractarians. I am afraid of giving a judgment on these men, but if I did not read 'judge not that ye be not judged,' I should assert them to be not only disingenuous and cowardly but false. . . . . These are my secret opinions—mind, I say opinions, not convictions."

May 23rd, 1842.—"I have read and studied some of the *Tracts*, and their poetry, and nouvellettes, which give glimpses into the ascetic tone of their writers' minds and serve as keys to the peculiar form of principles which they have adopted, and which is all wrong I believe before God. . . . . I fear lest these men should have bewildered you with their sophistries and their artful appeals to your veneration, imagination, and perception of the beautiful."

August, 1842.—"I read some of the sermons by authors of *Tracts for the Times* which you gave me. There is the same moaning piety in them, and something darker."

"Talking of the Tractators—so you still like their *tone!* and so do I. There is a solemn and gentleman-like, and gentle earnestness which is most beautiful, and which I wish I may ever attain. But you have just as much reason for following them or even reading them much on that account, as the moth has for fluttering round the candle because it is bright. The case is hackneyed but the analogy is perfect."

To turn now to the verdict of the greatest teacher

of the Church of England, in this or any age, the late Frederick Denison Maurice. His biographer records how, near the close of 1835, "He took a somewhat noteworthy walk to Clapham, to attend one of the meetings of the 'Clapham Sect,' as the Wilberforces, Thorntons, &c., of that day were called. He often spoke of his having taken Dr. Pusey's tract with him on a walk of the kind, and how as he went along it became more and more clear to him that it represented everything that he did not think and did not believe, till at last he sat down on a gate, in what were then the open fields of Clapham, and made up his mind that it represented the parting point between him and the Oxford School. He always spoke of it with a kind of shudder, as it were, of an escape from a charmed dungeon. 'They never have allowed anyone who has come within their meshes to escape,' was often his last sentence on the subject. I am pretty sure, however, that in thus speaking he was more especially thinking of some men who, having been under the 'Oxford' influence, have apparently altogether escaped from it, and that he meant that the effect upon their minds had never been effaced, no matter what opinions they subsequently adopted."

Early in the previous year, Mr. Maurice had penned some very characteristic words in reference to the Tractarian School:—"If they err and stumble in their sincere endeavours after the recovery of old and forgotten truths, if they even are tempted to forget that the Church is Catholic, while they are in the act of pleading for its Catholicity, if they do anything unwillingly to hurt that unity which they so earnestly contend for, may their oversights be all forgiven, all corrected, and may they daily advance more themselves, and lead others further in the knowledge of all truth."

Again Mr. Strachey, writing on October 27, 1836, says:—"I have heard Maurice say more in dispraise of the Oxford Church party since I came back than before. He regrets very much that they fancy themselves witnesses against the Evangelical (experimental) religionists and the Rationalists, thus becoming deniers instead of assertors. Maurice says that these men have not the least understanding of the use of the Reformation; they have no idea that it was a good thing, a stage in the scheme of the Divine education. And while they uphold the authority of the Church, and require men to receive its doctrines in childlike simplicity, they dislike it to be declared that these doctrines are the truth, and *therefore* were revealed by God before man could apprehend them by reason, preferring rather to take them as mere authoritative dogmas. Thus they would have the world ever continue in childhood, instead of advancing through boyhood and manhood; and they are unable to appreciate the two latter periods, or to see that in the last is the perfection of the first, which they exclusively value."

The biographer of the Rev. F. W. Robertson (of Brighton) tells us how he had been "much impressed by a sermon of Mr. Newman's on 'Sin after Baptism;' and the contest which arose in his mind from his sense of the fervour and sincerity of religious feeling which marked the Tract School, and his own instinctive recoil from the doctrines which they held, resulted in a state of deep mental depression." He also observes most truly that the almost fierceness with which Robertson speaks against the Tract School was a proof *in him* of the strength of the attraction it possessed for him.

In a letter to his father, written from Brasenose College, Oxford, in 1840, a few months before his ordina-

tion, the magnificent preacher of after years speaks thus of the influence which pervaded Oxford at that time:—
"But I seem this term to have in measure waked out of a long trance, partly caused by my own gross inconsistencies, and partly by the paralysing effects of this Oxford delusion—heresy, for such it is, I feel persuaded. And to know it a man must live here, and he will see the promising and ardent men sinking one after another in a deadly torpor, wrapped up in self-contemplation, dead to their Redeemer, and useless to his Church, under the baneful breath of this accursed upas tree."

While we have thus to admit that the movement, as a religious power influencing the general life of the Church of England, appeared in very different lights to various individuals of the highest personal character, and the most acute judgment, we are bound to consider its effect upon the University of Oxford as a seat of learning and a place of education.

It was said on behalf of the movement by Mr. William Palmer, in his narrative of events connected with it, that, "The complete organisation of the party and the amount of truth which underlay their system, produced great and permanent results in society. One of its benefits was the interest which it excited in the young in all religious practices and exercises. . . . . It . . . . promoted religious exercises and seriousness of character, and a keen interest on many religious questions which had been matters of indifference."

Let us turn, however, to the debit side of the account. A writer upon "Study and Opinion in Oxford" in *Macmillan's Magazine* for December, 1869, has said: "Tractarianism burst upon us with the blind force of a movement at once reform and reaction, strong in the very contrast of the spirituality of its leader and the unreasoning excitement of the bulk of his clerical and undergraduate followers. . . . . . It is enough to say that it gathered up in the theological interest almost the whole intellectual force of Oxford ; that everybody became a theologian ; and that what was not theology, or could not be pressed into its service, was condemned."

Writing in the same strain Mr. Pattison, who possessed the fullest opportunities for forming an accurate judgment, remarks : " It was soon after 1830 that the *Tracts* desolated Oxford life, and suspended, for an indefinite period, all science, humane letters, and the first strivings of intellectual freedom which had moved in the bosom of Oriel." In regard, however, to this aspect of the question we shall at present say no more, as our attention will be recalled to it, when reviewing the condition of Oriel College and the University at a later point in our narrative. Having thus in some slight measure sketched the general history of the Tract experiment, and the aspects in which its principles appeared to various distinguished persons, we shall be able to take up the thread of our narrative at the year 1833, and in the next chapter note some of the more striking incidents of the movement as far as the time of the great collapse in 1845.

TRACTS FOR THE TIMES, BY MEMBERS OF THE. UNIVERSITY OF OXFORD.

Vol. I. for 1883-34.

1 Thoughts on the Ministerial Commission, respectfully Addressed to the Clergy.
2 The Catholic Church.
3 Thoughts Respectfully Addressed to the Clergy on Alterations in the Liturgy.

THE TRACTARIAN UPHEAVAL. 107

4. Adherence to the Apostolical Succession the Safest Course.
5. A Short Address to his Brethren on the Nature and Constitution of the Church of Christ, and of the Branch of it Established in England. By a Layman.
6. The Present Obligation of Primitive Practice.
7. The Episcopal Church Apostolical.
8. The Gospel a Law of Liberty.
9. On Shortening the Church Service.
10. Heads of a Week-day Lecture, delivered to a Country Congregation in ——shire.
11. The Visible Church. Letters I. and II.
12. Bishops, Priests and Deacons.
13. Sunday Lessons—The Principle of Selection.
14. The Ember Days.
15. On the Apostolical Succession of the English Church.
16. Advent.
17. The Ministerial Commission a Trust from Christ for the Benefit of His People.
18. Thoughts on the Benefits of the System of Fasting Enjoined by our Church.
19. On Arguing Concerning the Apostolical Succession.
20. The same continued. Letter III.
21. Mortification of the Flesh a Scripture Duty.
22. The Athanasian Creed.
23. The Faith and Obedience of Churchmen the Strength of the Church.
24. The Scripture View of the Apostolic Commission.
25. Bishop Beveridge on the Great Necessity and Advantage of Public Prayer.
26. Bishop Beveridge on the Necessity and Advantage of Frequent Communion.
27. Bishop Cosin on the Doctrine of the Eucharist.
28. The same continued.
29. Christian Liberty; or, Why Should we Belong to the Church of England? By a Layman.

30 The same continued.
31 The Reformed Church.
32 The Standing Ordinances of Religion.
33 Primitive Episcopacy.
34 Rites and Customs of the Church.
35 The People's Interest in their Minister's Commission.
36 Account of Religious Sects at Present Existing in England.
37 Bishop Wilson's Form of Excommunication.
38 Via Media. No. 1.
39 Bishop Wilson's Form of Receiving Penitents.
40 Baptism.
41 Via Media. No. 2.
42 Bishop Wilson's Meditations on his Sacred Office. No. 1 —Sunday.
4 Length of the Public Service.
44 Bishop Wilson's Meditations on his Sacred Office. No. 2 —Monday.
45 The Grounds of Our Faith.
46 Bishop Wilson's Meditations on his Sacred Office. No. 3 Tuesday.

Vol. II., 1834-35.

47 The Visible Church. Letter IV.
48 Bishop Wilson's Meditations on his Sacred Office. No. 4 —Wednesday.
49 The Kingdom of Heaven.
50 Bishop Wilson's Meditations on his Sacred Office. No. 5 —Wednesday concluded.
51 On Dissent without Reason in Conscience.
52 Sermon for St. Matthias' Day. No. 1.
53 Bishop Wilson's Meditations on his Sacred Office. No. 5, Thursday.
54 Sermon for the Annunciation. No. 2.
55 Bishop Wilson's Meditations on his Sacred Office. No. 5, Thursday continued.

56 Holidays Observed in the English Church.
57 Sermon for St. Mark's Day. No. 3.
58 On the Church, as Viewed by Faith and by the World.
59 The Position of the Church of Christ in England Relatively to the State and the Nation.
60 Sermon for St. Philip and St. Jude. No. 4.
61 The Catholic Church a Witness against Illiberality.
62 Bishop Wilson's Meditations on his Sacred Office. No. 5, Thursday concluded.
63 The Antiquity of the Existing Liturgies.
64 Bishop Bull on the Ancient Liturgies.
65 Bishop Wilson's Meditations on his Sacred Office. No. 6, Friday and Saturday.
66 Thoughts on the Benefit of Fasting. Supplement to Tract 18.
67 Scriptural Views of Holy Baptism.
68 The same continued.
69 The same continued.
70 Notes to Scriptural Views of Holy Baptism.

Vol. III., 1835-1836.

71 On the Controversy with the Romanists.
72 Archbishop Ussher on Prayer for the Dead.
73 On the Introduction of Rationalistic Principles into Religion.
74 Catena Patrum. No. 1. Testimony of writers in the later English Church to the Doctrine of the Apostolical Succession.
75 On the Roman Breviary, as Embodying the Substance of the Devotional Services of the Church Catholic.
76 Catena Patrum. No. 2. Testimony of Writers in the Later English Church to the Doctrine of Baptismal Regeneration.
77 Preface, Title-page, and Contents to Volume III.

Vol. IV., 1836-37.

78 Catena Patrum. No. 3. Testimony of Writers in the Later English Church to the Duty of Maintaining Quod semper, Quod ubique, Quod ab omnibus traditum est.
79 On Purgatory. (Against Romanism. No. 3.)
80. On Reserve in Communicating Religious Knowledge. Part I. From the Example of Our Lord. Part II. From the Example of Our Lord confirmed by His Moral Government. Part III. Some Reflections on the foregoing observations.
81. Catena Patrum. No. 4. Testimony of Writers of the Later English Church to the Doctrine of the Eucharistic Sacrifice, with an Historical Account of the Changes made in the Liturgy as to the expression of that Doctrine.
82 The Preface, Title-page, and Contents to Volume IV.
83 Advent Sermon on Anti-Christ.
84 Whether a Clergyman of the Church of England be now bound to have Morning and Evening Prayer daily in his Parish Church.
85 Lectures on the Scripture Proofs of the Doctrines of the Church.
86 Indications of a Superintending Providence in the Preservation of the Prayer Book, and in the Changes it has undergone.
87 On Reserve in Communicating Religious Knowledge.
88 The Greek Devotions of Bishop Andrews translated and arranged.
89 On the Mysticism attributed to the Early Fathers in the Church.
90 Remarks on Certain Passages in the Thirty-nine Articles.

There were also published, contemporaneously with the *Tracts for the Times*, a number of short papers entitled

Records of the Church, consisting of translated extracts from the writings of the earliest Christian Fathers, and thus giving information at first hand about the sufferings and the doctrines of the Primitive Church.

Subjoined to each of the *Tracts for the Times* was a list of books commended to the reader in these terms:

"The following Works, all in single volumes, or pamphlets, and recently published, will be found more or less to uphold or elucidate the general doctrines inculcated in these *Tracts*."

The list comprised works by Bishop Taylor, Dr. Pusey, Mr. Newman, Mr. Keble, Bishop Jebb, Dr. Hook, Mr. Rose, etc., and attention was also directed to the larger standard works of Bishop Bull, Waterland, Wall, Pearson, Leslie, Bingham, Palmer and Hooker.

CHAPTER V.

THE PROGRESS OF THE UNDULATION.

At the beginning of the Long Vacation of 1833 the Rev. W. Palmer, of Worcester College, and Mr. Hurrell Froude met in the Common Room of Oriel, and resolved to form an association for vindicating the rights of the Church, and restoring the knowledge of what they believed to be sound principles. Mr. Palmer communicated the design to Mr. Rose, and Mr. Froude laid it before Mr. Keble. Mr. Newman was at that time absent, as we have seen, from England, but on his return in the course of a few weeks at once joined the association. Mr. Keble, writing to two friends in August, described the objects of the association as, firstly, the circulation of true or primitive notions about the Apostolical Succession, and secondly, the protection of the Prayer Book against profane innovation.

A few words must here be devoted to Mr. Palmer " He came from Trinity College, Dublin, to pursue inquiries, for which Oxford was a more congenial as well as convenient place. In his own preparation for holy orders he had had to study the Prayer Book, and for this purpose he found abundance of commentaries of a doctrinal and practical character. But he desired to learn the origin and history of our formularies, and for this he could find little or no help. So he came to Oxford. Fate, or the kindness of a friend, directed him to Worcester College ; choice took him often to Oriel. He had at once placed in his hands Bishop Lloyd's annotated folio Prayer Book, and an older document of the same kind in the Bodleian, besides other MSS. there. It should be said there had been a sort of revival of these studies a few years before. Shepherd, a promising young clergyman, had announced a Prayer Book with historical illustrations; and had set about it with industry, when he died. The very fragmentary work done was published by his sister, and several thousand guinea subscriptions testified to the interest felt even then in the antiquities of our ritual. Mr. Palmer brought out his *Origines Liturgica* in 1832, the year before the appearance of the *Tracts for the Times*. There is not a more interesting work to a scholar and divine, and hardly a more useful one to an ordinary clergyman."

"After residing some years at Oxford, taking the tenderest care of an aged mother, long the sole companion of his walks, Palmer left for a remote country living, and died, it may be said, in obscurity. Reward he wanted not, but he had not even recognition."

In the July of this year Mr. Hook, the future vicar of Leeds, had contributed to the *British Magazine*, edited at that time by Mr. Rose, a paper "in which the absurdity of Dr. Arnold's scheme for identifying Church and State by the simple expedient of including all denominations within the lines of the Church was ably exposed."

In the late summer or early autumn of this year *The Tracts for the Times*, or as *Aurora Leigh* terms them, "The Tracts Against the Times," first made their appearance. The first three of them are not dated, but No. 4 seems to have been written on September 21. The first was from Newman's pen, and began with words, the modesty yet solemnity of which could hardly fail to attract attention. "I am but one of yourselves, a Presbyter; and therefore I conceal my name, lest I should take too much on myself by speaking in my own person. Yet speak I must; for the times are very evil, yet no one speaks against them."

He goes on to speak of the duty laid upon the Clergy of supporting the Bishops, though of the latter he says, ominously enough :—" Black event as it would be, for the country, yet (as far as they are concerned) we could not wish them a more blessed termination of their course, than the spoiling of their goods and martyrdom."

This first tract endeavoured to stamp upon the minds of the clergy, to whom it was addressed, the thoughts of the Apostolical succession of the Bishops and the reality of their own spiritual commission. " The clergy everywhere took the cue, and the party ran the narrowest chance of being called, instead of calling itself, that of the Apostolicals."

When the *Tracts* had once begun to appear, Mr. Palmer, Mr. Perceval, and others were very anxious that they should be subjected to a committee of revision, that they might thus have the imprimatur of the whole association, but Mr. Newman, Mr. Keble, and Mr. Froude declined to consent; consequently the publication of the *Tracts* fell almost entirely into their hands, while Mr. Palmer and the other orthodox High and Dry Churchmen maintained a cautious but sympathetic attitude towards the movement. Mr. Palmer, however, during the autumn visited several large towns to secure the support of as many clergy as possible for the Association, a circular of which had been printed and circulated throughout England.

Mr. Newman's position at the start of the movement has been described by himself in effect as something of this sort: First, he was contending for the principle of dogma, his battle was with liberalism, understanding by liberalism the anti-dogmatic principle and its development. He says, "I have changed in many things; in this I have not. From the age of fifteen, dogma has been the fundamental principle of my religion; I know no other religion; I cannot enter into the idea of any other sort of religion; religion, as a mere sentiment, is to me a dream and a mockery. As well can there be filial love without the fact of a father, as devotion without the fact of a Supreme Being."

Secondly, he says, "I was confident in the truth of a certain definite religious teaching, based upon this foundation of dogma, viz., that there was a visible Church, with sacraments and rites which are the channels of invisible grace. I thought that this was the doctrine of Scripture of the early Church, and of the Anglican Church."

Thirdly, he founded the Episcopal system upon the Epistles of S. Ignatius.

Newman had ever a most serious sense of his own responsibility to his own Bishop, and has said, "I loved to act as feeling myself in my Bishop's sight, as if it were the sight of God. It was one of my special supports and safe-guards against myself; I could not go very wrong while I had reason to believe that I was in no respect displeasing him." . . . "This continued all through my course; when at length in 1845, I wrote to Bishop Wiseman, in whose vicariate I found myself, to announce my conversion, I could find nothing better to say to him than that I would obey the Pope as I had obeyed my own Bishop in the Anglican Church." Nothing is more striking in the history of the movement than the contrast between the attitude of the great leader to the spiritual powers that be, and that of the representatives of the party to-day. The ritualist of the last years of the century professes unbounded reverence for episcopacy in the abstract, but snaps his fingers, so far as he dare, at the decisions or requests of bishops in the concrete.

Again in 1833 Newman was distinctly anti-Roman in his views. He had been brought up to look upon the Pope as anti-Christ, and at Christmas, 1824, had preached a sermon to that effect. At the time when the movement began he considered that the Church of Rome was bound up with the cause of anti-Christ by the Council of Trent. Moreover, he tells us, "At least during the Tract movement, I thought the essence of her offence to consist in the honours which she paid to the blessed Virgin and the Saints; and the more I grew in devotion, both to the Saints and to our lady, the more impatient was I at the Roman practices, as if those glorified creations of God must be gravely shocked, if pain could be theirs, at the undue veneration of which they were the object."

Hurrell Froude, however, was always doing his best to obliterate this idea from Newman's mind, and in one of the early tracts published in 1834, the latter wrote as follows: "Considering the high gifts and the strong claims of the Church of Rome and its dependencies on our admiration, reverence, love and gratitude, how could we withstand it, as we do; how could we refrain from being melted into tenderness, and rushing into communion with it, but for the words of truth itself, which bids us prefer it to the whole world?"

The conflict at that time in Newman's case was between reason and affection, and his feeling he described to be "like that of a man, who is obliged in a court of justice to bear witness against a friend."

He felt such full certitude in the position of the Anglican Communion, and such confidence in the substantial justice of the charges which could be brought against Rome, that he did not hesitate to push forward principles which would certainly, if accepted, bring the Anglican system into closer conformity to that of the Latin Church.

Men said that what he and Froude were teaching was sheer popery. Newman answered, " True, we seem to be making straight for it; but go on awhile, and you will come to a deep chasm across the path, which makes real approximation impossible."

Newman made no attempt to systematise, or carefully define the work on which he found himself engaged with a number of associates. He adopted the principle of a loose formation, and thought it best that each of his co-workers should exhibit, in his own best way, whatever of light or wisdom there might be found in him. He says; " I felt great impatience at our being called a party, and would not allow that we were such. I had a lounging, free-and-easy way of carrying things on. I exercised no sufficient censorship upon the *Tracts*." ... " These, at first starting, were short, hasty, and some of them ineffective; and at the end of the year, when collected into a volume, they had a slovenly appearance."

It was under these circumstances that Dr. Pusey, towards the close of 1833, appeared disposed to throw in his lot with the new movement, and he was the man of all others in Oxford at that time whose support would seem desirable to the leaders.

Edward Bouverie Pusey was a member of an ancient Berkshire family, holding an estate at Pusey, in that county, by a horn, given, it is said, to their ancestors by Canute, the Danish king; a legend being preserved to this effect,—that an individual, who, in the disguise of a shepherd, had got into the enemy's camp, informed the king of an ambuscade formed by the Saxons to intercept him. E. B. Pusey took his B.A. degree from Christ Church, as a First Class Lit. Hum., in 1822. In the year 1824, having already obtained a Fellowship at Oriel, he won the University prize for the Latin Essay. During the next three or four years he resided chiefly at various German Universities, but returned to Oxford in 1828 as Regius Professor of Hebrew and Canon of Christ Church. On his return from the continent he published "An Historical Inquiry into the Probable Causes of the Rational Character lately Predominant in the Theology of Germany," this work was looked upon as, in some sort, an apology for German Theology in reply to the charge brought against it by Mr. Rose, the Christian Advocate for Cambridge, and it would seem that Pusey at that time entertained views on the sufficiency of Scripture and the authority of Tradition, which would have hardly been endorsed by the party of 1833, with whom we find him now allying himself. We find him, however, afterwards complaining of German "theories which pull to pieces what has been received for thousands of years."

Mr. Newman had known him well for some years, and had felt for him an enthusiastic admiration. Speaking of his adhesion to the movement he writes,—" His great learning, his immense diligence, his scholarlike mind, his simple devotion to the cause of religion, overcame me; and great, of course, was my joy, when, in the last days of 1833, he showed a disposition to make common cause with us. His Tract on Fasting appeared as one of the series, with the date of December 21. He was not, however, I think, fully associated in the movement till 1835 and 1836, when he published his Tract on Baptism, and started the Library of the Fathers. He at once gave us a position and a name. Without him we should have had little chance, especially at the early date of 1834, of making any serious resistance to the Liberal aggression. But Dr. Pusey was a Professor and Canon of Christ Church; he had a vast influence in consequence of his deep religious seriousness, the munificence of his charities, his professorship, his family connections, and his easy relations with University authorities. He was to the movement all that Mr. Rose might have been, with that indispensable addition, which was wanting to Mr. Rose, the intimate friendship and the familiar daily society of the persons who had commenced it." . . . . " He was a man of large designs ; he had a hopeful sanguine mind ; he had no fear of others ; he was haunted by no intellectual perplexities."

" Dr. Pusey's influence was felt at once. He saw that there ought to be more sobriety, more gravity, more careful pains, more sense of responsibility in the *Tracts* and in the whole movement. It was through him that the character of the *Tracts* was changed."

We have seen that the early numbers of the *Tracts* were short, hasty, and it may be said without injustice, reckless ; under Dr. Pusey's influence they became longer, more careful, more accurate, and more methodical.

In the early years, however, of the movement, Pusey's influence was not generally felt in the same way as that of Froude and Newman, nor is the reason far to seek ; they were men of genius, he was a laborious student ; they were in themselves far above and beyond their writings ; he was probably, in some measure, a disappointment to many who were drawn to seek him, having hitherto known him as one of the most profound, as well as voluminous religious writers of this age. Mr. Mozley tells us that "Pusey's voice might want music and flexibility, but, whatever the cause, it was a powerful engine."

The same may be said of the substance of his sermons. They are adorned by no eloquence, and are singularly destitute of grace and rhythm; but they are rich, for all that, in profound spiritual thought, with that combination of tenderness and severity which ever marks the utterances of a deeply serious character.

The most grave charge ever brought against Dr. Pusey, a charge incapable of investigation at the time when it was advanced, was contained in the publication, after his death, of the autobiography of Mr. Mark Pattison, who records how,—" I once, and only once, got so low by fostering a morbid state of conscience as to go to Confession to Dr. Pusey. Years afterwards it came to my knowledge that Pusey had told a fact about myself, which he got from me on that occasion, to a friend of his, who employed it to annoy me." We are inclined to think that those who knew Dr. Pusey best, will be most certain to think that Mr. Pattison made a grievous mistake, and gave the mistake publicity in an unjustifiable way.

It does not, however, become any historian, even the humblest, to speak of any human characters under consideration in terms either of unmitigated censure, or of undiscriminating praise. Nor can an exception be made even in such a slight sketch as the present, in dealing even with a personality so considerable as Dr. Pusey.

It is granted to but few spiritual leaders to escape altogether the snares of affectation or coxcombry, and

Dr. Pusey can hardly be numbered among those select few.

In his later years he would speak to pious ladies, in accents of tender regret, about the disappointment it had been to him that he had not been called to the performance of direct parochial work. Men of robust common sense cannot force themselves to forget that a number of English benefices are in the gift of Christ Church, and that if Dr. Pusey had really in spirit and in truth wished for a country living in preference to the office of Regius Professor, his longing might have been gratified without much difficulty.

Again, a writer in the *Church Quarterly Review* has described how : " Some saw him for the first time as he came forth from his widowed home. He was unlike any figure of sorrow they had ever beheld : shrunken, pale, withered, creeping through the chill air as if afraid to walk in a world to which he no more belonged. He climbed up the steps of the University pulpit as if he dreaded to look down on the sea of faces and meet their eyes, and he began to preach feebly, with a hollow voice, gathering volume as it went, in a crushed sepulchral tone, till every ear slowly vibrated with the monotone of his prayer, and every heart was hushed with a sense of awe as if it were made an involuntary witness of a man of affliction in his hour of loneliest communion with God. This was the impression made on many a young man fresh from the joyous success of life in a public school ; and no wonder that Oxford, with this occasional apparition of Dr. Pusey, presented to him an idea absolutely new." We can hardly consider Dr. Pusey well advised in having preached at all at such a time, or his Reviewer discreet in having described the circumstance in such terms.

There is a tone of greater and more simple reality in a passage from the pen of Sir J. T. Coleridge:—" Keble returned, it will be remembered, from his mother's death-bed to the Schools at Oxford, and continued in the discharge of his duty as examining master through the week until the day of her funeral. A young man had given in among his books some plays of Euripides, including the Alcestis. Keble happened to be conducting his examination; and whether inadvertently, or, as we sometimes do, humouring the sorrow at his heart, had set him on the part (ver. 395 et. seqq.), in which she dies in the presence of her husband, Admetus, her son Eumelus, and his sister. Much of the tenderness and pathos of the passage arises from the wonderful simplicity of the language, which it is almost impossible to reproduce in a translation;" .... " Keble, as was then usual, was standing; he heard the passage out with fixed attention, and unchanged countenance, then dropped on his chair, and burying his face in his hands on the table, remained for some time, silent, overcome with emotion."

It has been said by Mr. Mozley that "the year 1834, in respect of events, was as the calm which precedes the storm, but it was one of vast preparation and incessant labour. Nine or ten men were now doing their best to out-talk, and out-write, and out-manœuvre the world, and so heartily did they set about it that there ensued a certain degree of competition. There were writers who could write nothing short; writers who could write a good sonnet or an ode, but nothing in prose under a volume; and all disclosed a life of incubation. If one of them saw that his colleague had ventured on thirty pages, he would take sixty, and soon found himself exceeded by the same rule. The *Tracts* took time to write, and perhaps more time to read. Sermons were preached everywhere, even in the Chapel Royal, but mostly in country places, and published with long introductions and copious appendices. High and Low Church stood by amazed, and very doubtful what it would come to; but meanwhile equally pleased to see life in the Church, which the House of Commons seemed to think incapable of thought, will or action. The correspondence grew. Oxford resumed its historic place as the centre of religious activity. This was the golden age of the movement, and men talked rather gaily. Some readily accepted the charge of conspiracy, and were far from prompt to disavow that there was more in the background."

The biographer of Dr. Hook has told us how, in this year, " one of the most direct fruits of the Association was an address signed by about 7,000 of the clergy, and presented to the Archbishop of Canterbury (Howley) in February, 1834. This address was a declaration, that amidst the growth of Latitudinarian sentiments and ignorance concerning the spiritual claims of the Church, the signatories wished to express their devoted adherence to the apostolical doctrine and polity of the Church, and their deep-rooted attachment to the Liturgy as an embodiment of the primitive faith; but that while they deprecated any rash innovation in spiritual matters, the primate might rely upon their hearty and dutiful support in carrying into effect such wholesome reforms as the times might require, especially such as would tend to revive the discipline of ancient times, to strengthen the connection between the bishops, clergy, and people, and to promote the purity, efficiency, and unity of the Church."

To turn to the progress of the movement at Oxford,

Newman, in this year, driven perforce to assert his own intense individuality, published his first volume of *Parochial Sermons*. "It was as if a trumpet had sounded through the land. All read and admired, even if they dissented or criticised. The publishers said that the volume put all other sermons out of the market, just as *Waverley* and *Guy Mannering* put out all other novels. Sermons to force their way without solicitation, canvassing, subscription, or high-sounding recommendation, were unknown in those days, and these flew over the land." ... "But long before the publication of his sermons, Newman had gathered round him the best part of his own college and of some others—men to whom the sermons were the treat of the week, and who would often recall to one another the passages that had most struck them."

In this year, too, Newman began daily morning prayers at S. Mary's, and, in conjunction with Dr. Pusey, took a house at Oxford, in S. Aldate's, and established it as a kind of hostel for young graduates who might be willing to remain "up" to study divinity. After a couple of years, however, this new hall was found not to attract inmates, and Dr. Pusey generously received the surviving members under his own roof, some of them rendering a certain amount of assistance to Newman and himself in various literary projects.

Towards the end of 1834 the movement had to meet the first onset of the Liberal attack. Dr. Hampden, the Principal of S. Mary's Hall, and Professor of Moral Philosophy, "produced an able but startling pamphlet entitled 'Observations on Religious Dissent, with Particular Reference to the Use of Religious Tests in the University.' Without referring to the *Tracts for the Times*, or other publications of the day, he struck at the root of the movement; for he stated that the Creeds were but opinions, for which a man could not be answerable, and that they were expressed in obsolete phraseology. In this pamphlet, and in other forms there was now before the University a distinct proposal to abolish subscription to the Thirty-Nine Articles."

Shortly afterwards, Henry Wilberforce returned Hampden's fire in a very powerful letter to the Primate, entitled, "The Foundation of the Faith Assailed in Oxford." Nothing, however, very definite resulted from the encounter.

The year 1835 witnessed the steady rise in the tide of the movement. It found Hurrell Froude "contributing to the *Tracts* from Barbadoes, and also freely criticising them when they seemed to him to temporise or to fall into modern conventionalisms. In fact, he was keeping Newman, nothing loth, up to the mark. In May, 1835, he returned from Barbadoes. On landing he found a letter from Newman calling him to Oxford, where there were several friends, soon to part for the Long Vacation. His brother Anthony was summoned from his private tutor, Mr. Hubert Cornish. Froude came, full of energy and fire, sunburnt, but a shadow. The tale of his health was soon told. He had a 'button in his throat,' which he could not get rid of, but he talked incessantly. With a positive hunger for intellectual difficulties, he had been studying Babbage's calculating machine, and he explained, at a pace which seemed to accelerate itself, its construction, its performances, its failures, and its certain limits. Few, if any, could follow him; still less could they find an opening for aught they had to say, or to beg a minute's law. He never could realise the laggard pace of duller intelligences."

During this year Newman's attention was largely occupied in the building of a Church at Littlemore, a hamlet some three miles from Oxford, attached to the living of S. Mary's. Newman often walked over there, and his mother and sisters had already taken charge of the school and the poor. "Newman's own ideas of a village church were simple, almost utilitarian. So little part had he in the great ecclesiological and ritual revival, which has changed not only the inside of our churches, but the face of the land, that from first to last he performed the service after the fashion of the last century. At his own church of S. Mary's was retained the custom, said to be from Puritan times, of handing the sacred elements to the communicants at their places down the long chancel, the desks of which, covered with white linen for the occasion, looked much like tables. All he wanted at Littlemore was capacity and moderate cost." The first stone was laid in July, 1835, and the church was completed and consecrated in the following year. The work was so plain throughout as hardly to satisfy even the builder or glazier, one of whom inserted, on his own authority, a single suggestive piece of red glass high up in the middle lancet of the east window. This was accepted by the *Record* as symbolic of the Saviour's blood.

The next three or four years, however, witnessed an advance in the Littlemore arrangement, the church receiving fresh additions to its furniture, viz.: "two candlesticks (with their candles), from the patterns at Magdalen College, and a large paten in the centre, a neat desk of carved oak, to represent the black eagle, from which the lessons are read, besides sundry hieroglyphics of pelicans, etc., on the ornamental shields attached to the ends of the rafters in the roof, and the whole service partaking of the symbolical character of the Roman-Catholic ritual, the officiating minister turning at one time to the people, and gently lifting his hands in token of the blessings conveyed; at other times to the East, and bending towards the cross makes the genuflexion, etc." It was reported among the villagers that the above-mentioned hieroglyphics had been presented to their Vicar by the Queen!

Probably, however these slight ritual developments at Littlemore were due to the influence of Newman's friends rather than to his own unbiassed preferences. It must be said both for him and Pusey that their minds were not devoted to small observances. It was remarked about the time of the death of the latter, by one of the leading dailies, that a pilgrim to the Parish Church at Pusey might very possibly even then find the rite of Baptism administered out of a cracked slop-bason. And Dr. Pusey has recorded how Newman, as vicar of S. Mary's, retained the napkins which he found on the altar.

The most important publication of the Party of the Movement during 1835 was Dr. Pusey's series of four tracts on Baptism, which were regarded by Frederick Denison Maurice as the true representative notes of the party as a party. " He said, for instance, in later life that their publication and their importance in relation to the Movement justified the statement made by Dr. Newman in his *Apologia* that Dr. Pusey's joining him and his friends had given, to what had been beforehand a mere gathering together of sympathisers, weight and authority. What expressed to him the distinction between his view and Dr Pusey's was the statement that Dr. Pusey regarded 'Baptismal Regeneration' as a change of nature whilst he regarded it as the coming out of the infant under the first influence of a light which had always been shining for it and all the world." Speaking of the same publication, Dr. Hook wrote to S. Wilberforce:— "Pusey's tract on Baptism I admire extremely; it seems to me to contain more useful matter than any work that has been published in these latter days; but with respect to his notion of sin after Baptism, it does, between ourselves, approach in my opinion to Novatianism. It is a dreadful doctrine: I hope it is not true; I believe it is not—from the best attention I have been able to give to the subject, I think it is not."

In January, 1836, Hurrell Froude's end was at last, seen to be near, and he passed away on February 28th.

Bishop Wilberforce, writing to Miss Noel, alludes to it thus: "Did you hear anything of Froude's death, of the quietness and peace with which that mighty intellect left its tabernacle as if it had been the departing breath of a fainting child—on a Sunday—when his father had read the Liturgical Service with him, and had just finished a sermon. He was, I think, upon the whole, possessed of the most original powers of thought of any man I have ever known intimately." The death of Mr. Froude seems to have drawn Mrs. Keble's mind to the thought of the Communion of Saints; we find her writing on March 9th: "I can't help thinking, at least one doesn't know, but that Mr. Froude may in some way or other be of more service now, than if he had been kept here longer."

It must be borne in mind that a strongly-revived belief in the living union of the faithful with those who have passed hence, is one of the abiding spiritual results of the movement.

Dr. Newman has told us how "On Hurrell Froude's death, in 1836, I was asked to select one of his books as a keepsake. I selected Butler's *Analogy;* finding that it had been already chosen, I looked with some perplexity along the shelves as they stood before me, when an intimate friend at my elbow said, 'Take that.' It was the Breviary which Hurrell had had with him at Barbadoes. Accordingly I took it, studied it, wrote my tract from it, and have it on my table in constant use till this day."

In the spring of this same year Mr. Newman published in the *British Magazine*, a paper entitled "Home Thoughts Abroad," in which, as in other writings of his whilst an Anglican, the argument on behalf of Rome was stated with considerable force. He thus describes the reception with which it was met. "At the time my friends and supporters cried out 'How imprudent!' and, both at the time, and especially at a later date, my enemies have cried out, 'How insidious!'"

"Friends and foes virtually agreed in their criticism; I had set out the cause which I was combating to the best advantage: this was an offence; it might be from imprudence, it might be with a traitorous design. It was from neither the one nor the other; but for the following reasons. First, I had a great impatience, whatever was the subject, of not bringing out the whole of it as clearly as I could; next I wished to be as fair to my adversaries as possible; and thirdly I thought that there was a great deal of shallowness among my own friends, and that they undervalued the strength of the argument in behalf of Rome, and that they ought to be roused to a more exact apprehension of the position of the controversy." Mr. Newman at that time supposed that he had clearly before his mind the whole state of the question, on which the decision between the claims of the Anglican and Roman Churches depended. He regarded the strong point of the Anglican position to lie in the argument from Primitiveness, *i.e.*, in being able to show that Anglican doctrines and practices corresponded more nearly than the Roman to those of the Primitive Church. He admitted that the Roman ground was the stronger on the question of Universality, *i.e.*, a larger number of nationalities were in communion with Rome than with Canterbury.

However as time went on Mr. Newman came to feel that the argument from antiquity was not only the special plea of Anglicans, but also *their only one*. He also felt that the *Via Media*, which was his ideal of a true Church, half way between Romanism and bare Protestantism—and which he took to represent the Divine idea of the Church of England—was to be a sort of remodelled and adapted antiquity.

The most stirring event, however, of 1836, was the appointment of Dr. Hampden to the Regius Professorship of Divinity at Oxford. As soon as it became know that Hampden had been nominated by Lord Melbourne, his Bampton Lectures of 1832, which had hitherto been little read, began to attract attention. Their tendency was discovered to be dangerously Latitudinarian and Liberal, and consequently his appointment to such a position of trust called forth loud and angry protests. A large meeting of the Orthodox leaders was held in the common room of Corpus Christi College. It was soon seen that it was useless to attempt to stop the appointment, and that nothing remained but to obviate, as far as possible, its most mischievous consequences. It was proposed and carried that the Convocation of the University should deprive the Regius Professor for the time being, of the right to assist in nominating the select preachers, and also of his place as one of the judges to try any case of heresy.

A meeting of Convocation was summoned, to which the clergy swarmed up from all parts of England.

The vote of exclusion or deprivation was carried by the Doctors and Masters, but was vetoed by the two Proctors, as had indeed been expected. A few weeks later, when fresh Proctors had come into office, another Convocation was convened and the vote was carried.

The triumphant majority, however, had won a victory which was sure in time to provoke retaliation; Hampden had been condemned, and the day was not far distant when the same measure would be dealt out to to some of his opponents. Many of the country clergy on this occasion openly expressed their hope that, the next time they were summoned to Oxford, it might be for the purpose of putting down the *Tracts*.

The opposition to Hampden's appointment attracted a good deal of notice in the country. The existence of a great cause and work at Oxford could no longer be ignored. Many influential clergy came to Oxford to investigate the movement for themselves.

During this year, too, Newman began a course of extempore lectures on ecclesiastical subjects, hardly suitable for the pulpit, in Adam de Broome's Chapel, an aisle partitioned off from S. Mary's.

From this time, for the next few years, his connection with Oriel gradually relaxed, he was "in the College but hardly of it, avoiding the common room, though having a common breakfast with two or three friends."

But at this time "nobody in Oxford was seeing so many people, and such a variety of people of such significance in the matter of religion, as Newman."

In the same year Dr. Pusey advertised his great

project for a translation of the fathers, and Dr. Wiseman, a distinguished Roman Monsignore, subsequently a Cardinal, at that time President of the *Collegio Inglese* at Rome, anticipating what was coming, returned to England, and delivered in London some note-worthy lectures on the doctrines of Catholicism.

The late Lord Houghton, speaking of Wiseman coming to England in later years, " the first Roman Cardinal that had stood on British soil since Pole had died amid the fires of Smithfield, with the missive from the Flaminian Gate in his hand," used words which may, in some measure, be fitly applied to his visit in 1836. " Again the extent and power of the High Church party that had lately developed itself at Oxford was extravagantly exaggerated by the Catholics, both at home and at Rome. The entirely intellectual character of the movement, and the certainty of its indignant repulse the moment it came into contact with the habits, instincts, and traditions of the English people, were not perceptible to Dr. Wiseman." In after years he had friendly relations with some members of the Tractarian party, "and he had been one of the first of the authorities of his Church to approach them with a sympathetic interest, and to attract them to what he believed the only safe conclusion by a kindly appreciation of their doubts and difficulties."

At this time, however, it was in view of Wiseman's London lectures that Newman was stirred to write his work on the *Prophetical office of the Church viewed relatively to Romanism and Popular Protestantism*, which was published in 1837. The author thus describes its scope and object : " It attempts to trace out the rudimental lines on which Christian faith and teaching proceed, and to use them as means of determining the relation of the Roman and Anglican systems to each other. In this way it shows that to confuse the two together is impossible, and that the Anglican can be as little said to tend to the Roman as the Roman to the Anglican." .... "But this volume had a larger scope than that of opposing the Roman system. It was an attempt at commencing a system of theology on the Anglican idea, and based upon Anglican. Mr. Palmer, about the same time, was projecting a work of a similar nature in his own way. It was published, I think, under the title, *A Treatise on the Christian Church*. As was to be expected from the author, it was a most learned, most careful composition; and in its form, I should say, polemical." Palmer's work was exact and methodical, "cutting the ground of controversy into squares, and giving each objection its answer," and was thus the book for theological students. Newman's work was experimental and tentative, he "wished to build up an Anglican theory out of the stores which already lay cut and hewn upon the ground, the past toil of great divines."

The subject of the volume was the *Via Media*, which, however positive a religious system it might be, Newman still admitted to be not as yet objective and real, to have, in fact, scarcely any existence except on paper. He says: "I wanted to bring out in a substantive form a living Church in England, in a position proper to herself, and founded on distinct principles: a living Church, made of flesh and blood, with voice, complexion, and motion, and action, and a will of its own. I believe I had no private motive, and no personal aim."

In this same year, 1837, Newman also wrote his *Essay on Justification*. "It was aimed at the Lutheran dictum that justification by faith only was the cardinal doctrine of Christianity."

Writing of this period, Mr. Mozley tells us that, "By the end of 1837 the 'movement' had diffused itself all over England. Every month there was a new sensation, and a new controversy.".... "The opponents of the movement, one and all, pronounced us on our way to Rome. Certainly very few of us could say where we meant to stop, or what we had in view as to the future of the Church of England. For my own part I never knew where it was all to end, except somewhere in the first three centuries of the Church, and I have to confess that I knew very little about them. Happily for us the case of our opponents was not a bit better than our own They they did not know where they stood, or what they would have, or where they tended to."

"But while the central agitation was telling on the whole of the country, it became itself the object of reciprocal influences. Everybody who had a want, everybody who had a difficulty, everybody who had a quarrel, everybody who could not do what he wanted to do, wrote to Newman, or to one of his friends, or to an editor, or an author, or simply to a man at Oxford."

Meanwhile "Newman had no college, office, or work, and was seldom seen in hall; but he gave receptions every Tuesday evening in the common room, largely attended by both the college and out-college men."

The year 1838 found the plot rapidly thickening. Newman, Keble, and Pusey undertook together to bring out a Library of the Fathers, in which they proposed to edit translations of the whole, or of selected portions of the writings of certain Fathers who had flourished previous to the division of Christendom into East and West. Though making themselves generally responsible,

THE TRACTARIAN UPHEAVAL. 135

they had to rely for its execution on the help of a number of gentlemen, many of them men of mark, and well known both at Oxford and Cambridge.

They themselves declined all pecuniary profit. Newman also this year published a pamphlet containing an attempt at putting the doctrine of the Real Presence on an intellectual basis; the fundamental idea being a denial of the existence of space, except as a subjective idea of our minds.

This year witnessed the first burst of the storm which the Movement provoked, and which resulted, a few years later, in the withdrawal of the great leader to another communion.

Dr. Faussett, the Margaret Professor of Divinity, a man of no great learning, but a clever writer and a telling preacher, delivered, and published on May 20, a sermon on the Revival of Popery. " He had carefully culled from Newman's writings, from the *Tracts for the Times*, but most of all from Froude's *Remains*, all the expressions used by writers more anxious to speak to the full extent of their feelings and convictions than to regard the perplexity or the pain they might inflict on some readers."

Dr. Hook, writing of this attack, remarks, "I am not any more than Dr. —— inclined to approve of Mr. Froude's *Remains*. I deeply, indeed, regret the publication of that work without a protest on the part of the editor against the author's many paradoxical positions. With a kind heart and glowing sensibilities, Mr. Froude united a mind saturated with learning, but from its very luxuriance productive of weeds together with many flowers. Though he always took an original, he sometimes took a morbid, view of things, and while from his writings all must derive much food for thought, from many of his opinions the majority of his readers will, like myself, dissent." . . . "Had Dr. —— contented himself with writing a pamphlet or a review, while we might have considered him incompetent to sit in judgment on such a mind as Mr. Froude's, we should have had no cause of complaint. But cause of complaint the Church has when he makes one work a pretext for attacking certain of his clerical brethren, whose learning he may be unable to appreciate, but whose piety and zeal he would do well to imitate."

Not long afterwards the charge of Dr. Bagot, the Bishop of Oxford, was published; and its sober judgments and fatherly tone stood out in pleasing contrast with the indiscriminating invectives of Dr. Faussett. Mr. Newman, however, attached considerable weight to the utterances of his diocesan, and at once offered to stop the *Tracts for the Times.* He wrote to Dr. Bagot in these terms, "I should feel a more lively pleasure in knowing that I was submitting myself to your Lordship's expressed judgment in a matter of that kind, than I could have even in the widest circulation of the volumes in question." The Bishop, however, did not at that time think it necessary that the *Tracts* should be stopped.

The weak point in Dr. Faussett's case was that, "All that he had done to check rationalism during the ten years he had held the chair was to deliver two sermons, neither of them quite fit for a Christian pulpit, and both calculated to give pain and do nothing more."

One of the sensations of this year was Hook's memorable sermon on "Hear the Church," preached before the Queen and her Court at the Chapel Royal. The sermon had an enormous circulation, and occasioned a great deal of discussion. The sermon was an old one, having been preached at Coventry, Leeds and elsewhere, but as Mr. Mozley justly remarks, "You may safely tell village and even town congregations that Saul was bound to obey Samuel, and David to accept the rebuke of Nathan and the judgment of Gad. It is another matter when you are addressing a Queen, and when the question of the day is, who is Samuel, who is Nathan, and who is Gad?"

The Queen was said to have been much pleased with the sermon; for that very reason, perhaps, her advisers were not pleased. "They had to square matters with the Church of England, the Church of Scotland, the Irish Catholics, and the English dissenters, and they did not feel themselves assisted by a peremptory command from the pulpit of the Chapel Royal to hear the only true Church, viz.: the Church of England."

There were, however, all manner of contradictory reports floating, at the time, as to her Majesty's attitude towards the sermon. S. Wilberforce made about this time the following entry in his diary in reference to it, "Heard afterwards that the Queen was very angry at it."

Towards the close of this year the Martyr's Memorial to Ridley, Cranmer and Latimer was got up at Oxford. Pusey and Newman set themselves against it, it being popularly regarded as, in some measure, intended to be a slap at Froude's *Remains*.

In 1838 Newman had felt himself obliged to decline further contributions from S. Wilberforce, the future Bishop of Oxford, to the *British Critic*, of which he was now editor, on the score of not feeling sure of Wilberforce's general approval of the body of opinions held by Pusey and himself. This refusal had possibly something to do with the gradual widening of the rift between the attractive rector of Brightstone and the leaders of the Movement.

The year 1839 was chiefly remarkable for the first serious doubt, which then arose in Newman's mind, as to the perfect security of the Anglican position. He writes :—" In the spring of 1839 my position in the Anglican Church was at its height. I had supreme confidence in my controversial *status*, and I had a great and still growing success in recommending it to others. I had in the foregoing autumn been somewhat sore at the Bishop's charge, but I have a letter which shows that all annoyance had passed from my mind. In January, if I recollect aright, in order to meet the popular clamour against myself and others, and to satisfy the Bishop, I had collected into one all the strong things which they, and especially I, had said against the Church of Rome, in order to their insertion among the advertisements appended to our publications."

The present writer has in his possession a bulky pamphlet, in the form of a letter from Dr. Pusey to the Bishop of Oxford, on the "Tendency to Romanism imputed to Doctrines held of Old, as Now, in the English Church." Bound up with this letter is an Appendix consisting of Extracts from the principal Tractarian Works showing their hostility to the Popish system. It would seem that this Appendix was drawn up by Newman, and was referred to in the above passage from the *Apologia*.

In the April number of the *British Critic* there appeared an article from Newman's pen, entitled "The State of Religious Parties," of which he says that "it contains the last words which I ever spoke as an Anglican to Anglicans. It may now be read as my parting address and valediction made to my friends. I little knew it at the time. It reviews the actual state of things, and it ends by looking towards the future."

In the course, however, of the next few months Newman received a mental shock, from which he never wholly recovered. About the middle of June he began to study the history of the Monophysites, and it was during this course of reading, which lasted for rather more than two months, that a doubt first came upon him about the tenableness of Anglicanism. He says— "My stronghold was antiquity; now here in the middle of the fifth century I found, as it seemed to me, Christendom of the sixteenth and nineteenth centuries reflected. I saw my face in that mirror, and I was a Monophysite. The Church of the *Via Media* was in the position of the Oriental Communion, Rome was where she now is, and the Protestants were the Eutychians." .... "It was difficult to make out how the Eutychians or Monophysites were heretics, unless Protestants and Anglicans were heretics also; difficult to find arguments against the Tridentine Fathers, which did not tell against the Fathers of Chalcedon; difficult to condemn the Popes of the sixteenth century without condemning the Popes of the fifth. The drama of religion, and the combat of truth and error, were ever one and the same. The principles and proceedings of the Church now were those of the Church then; the principles and proceedings of heretics then were those of Protestants now. I found it so—almost fearfully; there was an awful similitude, more awful, because so silent and unimpassioned, between the dead records of the past and the feverish chronicle of the present. The shadow of the fifth century was on the sixteenth. It was like a spirit rising from the troubled waters of the old world, with the shape and lineaments of the new. The Church then, as now, might be called peremptory and stern, resolute, overbearing and relentless; and heretics were shifting, changeable, reserved and deceitful, ever courting civil power, and never agreeing together, except by its aid; and the civil power was ever aiming at comprehensions, trying to put the invisible out of view, and substituting expediency for faith."

Hardly had Newman brought this course of reading to a close, when the August number of the *Dublin Review* was put into his hands by friends, more inclined to Rome than he was then himself.

It contained an article on the "Anglican Claim," by Dr. Wiseman, in which he considered the case of the Donatists and applied it to Anglicanism.

Newman at first did not see the cogency of the argument till a friend pointed out the words of Augustine, alluded to in the *Review*, which had escaped his observations, "*Securus judicat orbis terrarum.*" We may render the words in this connection as follows—The judgment of the Universal Church is sure. Newman's friend repeated the words again and again, and when he was gone, they kept ringing in his ears. "They decided ecclesiastical questions on a simpler rule than that of Antiquity; nay, St. Augustine was one of the prime oracles of Antiquity; here then was Antiquity deciding against itself." . . . . "The deliberate judgment, in which the whole Church at length rests and acquiesces, is an infallible prescription and a final sentence against such portions of it as protest and secede." . . . . "By those great words of the Ancient Father, interpreting and summing up the long and varied course of ecclesiastical history, the theory of the *Via Media* was absolutely pulverized."

Newman having mentioned the impression which this new view had made on him to two intimate friends, after a while got calm, and at length its vividness faded away. Meanwhile, however, he tells us—" I had seen the shadow of a hand upon the wall. It was clear that I had a good deal to learn on the question of the churches, and that perhaps some new light was coming upon me. He who has seen a ghost, cannot be as if he had never seen it. The heavens had opened and closed again. The thought for the moment had been, ' The Church of Rome will be found right after all;' and then it had vanished. My old convictions remained as before." He determined to be guided by the finger of God, and so far as he must perforce choose his own path, to be led by reason rather than by imagination.

Still, though Newman now felt that the theory of the *Via Media* had broken down, and his " Prophetical Office" had come to pieces, the argument against Rome, on the score of her practical errors, appeared to him as strong as ever. He found himself, from this time forward, more and ever more averse to speaking against the Roman Church herself, or her formal doctrines; but in consequence of this very feeling he found himself driven to insist upon the iniquity of " the political conduct, the controversial bearing, and the social methods and manifestations of Rome." Mr. O'Connell was at this time, so it seemed to Newman, advancing Catholicism by violence and intrigue, at the expense of the Anglican Church, and with the support of English Romanists.

On Newman's return to Oxford in October, 1839, he found that the hastiness and indiscretion of some of his followers were beginning to compromise him both with the Bishop of Oxford and with the University

Authorities, and that the article in the *Dublin Review* had made a considerable, and an uncomfortable, impression on others besides himself.

Towards the close of 1839, and during the following year, he set himself to examine carefully what could be said for the Anglican Church, in spite of its many short comings, in answer to Dr. Wiseman; and published an article on "The Catholicity of the English Church" in the *British Critic*, of January, 1840.

Newman saw clearly about this time that he must reckon seriously with the Thirty-Nine Articles of the Church of England. He felt that if the Church of England be indeed a true branch of the Primitive Church, it is necessary to show that the doctrines of the Primitive Church still lived in the Articles of her Belief. He felt "Man had done his worst to disfigure, to mutilate the old Catholic truth; but there it was in spite of them, in the Articles still. It was there, but this must be shown. It was a matter of life and death to us to show it."

Newman's attempt to show it took the form of the most notorious tract of all, No. 90, which was not, however, published till 1841, and which we shall consider more at length on a subsequent page.

In the year 1840, with which we are at present concerned, Newman began to contemplate the resignation of S. Mary's, and as a first step meditated a retirement to Littlemore; in fact, he went there to pass the Lent of 1840, and gave himself up to teaching in the Parish School, and practising the choir. Speaking of this time, he says:—"At the same time I had in view a Monastic house there. I bought ten acres of ground and began planting: but this great design was never carried out. I mention it, because it shows how little

I had really the idea at that time of ever leaving the Anglican Church."

He contemplated giving up S. Mary's, first on the score of being out of touch with the parishioners, and under the feeling that he had been using the Church as a means of influencing the University rather than a parochial charge. One instance, however, given by Mr. Mozley, goes to show that Newman's work as a Parish Priest in Oxford was not altogether null and void.

"He and his friends had declared strongly against the New Marriage Act, which relieved dissenters of the necessity of coming to Church to be married, but did not relieve the clergy of the necessity of marrying them, if they preferred to come to Church for that particular occasion. He suddenly found himself called on to perform the marriage service for one of the pretty daughters of a respectable pastry cook in S. Mary's parish. The family were Baptists, and the young lady was not baptized. Newman ascertained this by inquiry, and refused to perform the service, or to allow the marriage in his Church. The University was shocked at his inhumanity on such an occasion. Not so the young lady herself. She immediately expressed her wish to be baptized, declaring she was glad of the opportunity. She was baptized and married; and became an attached member of Newman's congregation, followed in time by the whole family."

For another reason, however, Newman wished to retire from the Church, which he expressed thus in a letter to Mr. Keble:—"The authorities of the University, the appointed guardians of those who form great part of the attendants on my sermons, have shown a dislike of my preaching. One dissuades men from coming; the late Vice-Chancellor threatens to take his own children away from the Church; and the present, having an opportunity last spring of preaching in my parish pulpit, gets up and preaches against the doctrine with which I am in good measure identified."

Mr. Keble dissuaded Newman from resigning S. Mary's at that time, on the ground that it might give people still further ground for suspecting that he was tending towards Rome. But from this time Newman employed a curate at S. Mary's, who gradually took more and more of the work.

How far Newman was in that year from any intention of "going over," may have been seen from words, written by him in the *British Critic*:—" We see it attempting to gain converts among us by unreal representations of its doctrines, plausible statements, bold assertions, appeals to the weaknesses of human nature, to our fancies, our eccentricities, our fears, our frivolities, our false philosophies. We see its agents smiling and nodding and ducking to attract attention, as gipsies make up to truant boys, holding out tales for the nursery, and pretty pictures, and gilt gingerbread, and physic concealed in jam, and sugar-plums for good children. Who can but feel shame when the religion of Ximenes, Barromes, and Pascal, is so overlaid." . . . " Till she ceases to be what she practically is, a union is impossible between her and England."

The chief publication of this year, 1840, on the lines of the Movement was Mr. Isaac Williams' tract on " Reserve in Communicating Religious Knowledge " This was one of the most remarkable and characteristic of the whole series of *The Tracts for the Times*, and one of those which awakened the most suspicion and opposition.

Mr. Mozley tells us how "Isaac Williams was the simplest of men. He had the happiness to live among friends with whom he entirely agreed; whom he loved and admired; whose sympathy almost excluded the outer world, and whose loyalty and power made him indifferent to vulgar opinions. Whatever he had said, or his friends had said, wisely and truly enough, he proclaimed from the housetop. In some respects this was the common temptation and the common fault of all the writers. Moving in a phalanx, with a certainty of support, they all said with tenfold freedom and fulness what they would have thought a good deal more about had they been called on to do it singly on their own separate account."

He got hold, in this instance, of a difficult and delicate subject, treated it with great ability on its positive side, but did not give much attention to compensating circumstances of considerable weight. He rightly insisted that our Lord and His Apostles carefully adapted their teaching to the state of knowledge, and the personal character of whose to whom they spoke. He neglected to note the changed conditions effected by the universal diffusion of the Bible. The printing press knocked reserve on the head.

The public has the Bible in its hands, and can find out for itself whether the book is simple and straightforward, or whether it abounds in mysteries and paradoxes The teacher of religion has then his choice, in case of question about any difficulty, either to say to the enquirer—"I will try to explain the difficulty to the best of my power," or "I question whether you are in a fit spiritual state to receive this hidden truth aright; I will wait till I know a little more about you."

It is not difficult to see to what mischievous ends any

doctrine of reserve might be manipulated by unscrupulous, or dishonest, religious teachers; how on the one hand it might be used to justify unworthy and unwarrantable concealment, and on the other to foster the spiritual pride of a select inner circle of attached followers. In the former sense it has been used, only too often, by Anglican directors to justify themselves in drawing young persons into the Confessional, without the knowledge of their parents, under the plea that the parents were not sufficiently educated in spiritual things to see the matter in the right light.

In the latter sense the abuse of reserve has justified the charge sometimes brought against the Tractarian movement of being essentially aristocratic in its tendency. It is natural for a priest to take a pride in being able to create a spiritual aristocracy in his parish; it is equally natural for the select few to feel flattered at being led along paths of spiritual knowledge which are closed to the vulgar many.

It was this aspect of the case to which Charles Kingsley referred when he wrote:—" So far from siding with Dr. —— he is, in my eyes, one of the most harmful men now in England; and .... in spite of his real holiness and purity, is not the man to whom I would entrust anyone I love. In him, and in all that school, there is an element of foppery—even in dress and manner; a fastidious, maundering, die-away effeminacy, which is mistaken for purity and refinement; and I confess myself unable to cope with it, so alluring is it to the minds of an effeminate and luxurious aristocracy; neither educated in all that should teach them to distinguish between bad and good taste, healthy and unhealthy philosophy and devotion. I never attempted but once to rescue a woman out of ——'s hands, and then I failed utterly and completely. I could not pamper her fancies as he could; for I could not bid her be more than a woman, but only to be a woman. I could not promise a safe and easy royal road to lily crowns, and palms of virginity, and the especial coronet of saints. I have nothing especial to offer anyone, except especial sorrow and trouble, if they wish to try to do especial good. I wish for no reward, no blessing, no name, no grace, but what is equally the heritage of pot-boys and navvies, and which they can realize and enjoy just as deeply as I can, while they remain pot boys and navvies, and right jolly ones too."

"Now this whole school (though there is much very noble and good in it, and they have re-called men's minds—I am sure they have mine—to a great deal of Catholic and apostolic truth which we are now forgetting) is an aristocratic movement in the fullest and most carnal sense. It is a system for saving the souls of fine ladies and gentlemen in an elegant and gentlemanlike way; for making it, the more riches they have, the more easy to enter into what they call the kingdom of heaven, and after sitting on high above the masses here on earth, to sit on high above them for ever hereafter."

Dr. Hook writes as follows on the subject:—"I wish Williams would explain himself more fully as regards his tract. It is one of the most beautiful, one of the most delightful tracts ever written; but in the third part he might moderate considerably. Surely there is a difference to be observed in our conduct in a nation which is heathen, and a nation by baptism made Christian; in a nation where heathenism is the traditional religion, and in a nation where the traditional religion is Christianity. The secret doctrines of our faith *are* in this country known; it is no longer a question whether they should be declared or not—that point is settled for us. Surely we are justified in taking care that they are not misapplied. I believe Williams would agree in all this; but he might very profitably explain himself more fully."

It may be interesting now to consider how it had been faring with Oriel, the birthplace of the movement, during the last ten years. It will be remembered that in the year 1830, Newman and Hurrell Froude had found themselves obliged to retire from the tutorship of the College, owing to serious differences with Dr. Hawkins, the Provost. During the years which followed Newman had "aimed at a moulding of the College of Fellows—there were at this date eighteen fellowships—on a mediæval system; at reviving the College of Adam de Brome and Laud, and mounting it as a reactionary machine to resist the formidable progress of 'Liberalism' and the modern spirit. The elections were to be so manipulated that a body of like-minded fellows should be obtained, who should all reside and study the Fathers, not necessarily occupying themselves with tuition. They would form a nucleus of learned controversialists, destined to fight against the vicious tendencies of an unbelieving age.

"The elections to fellowships for the ten years, from about 1830, were struggles between Newman endeavouring to fill the College with men likely to carry out his ideas, and the Provost endeavouring, upon no principle, merely to resist Newman's lead. Newman did not lose sight of the old Oriel principle of electing for promise rather than for performance; only, instead of looking for promise of originality, he now looked for promise of congeniality. Anyhow, in these contests, the old character of the Oriel fellowship was obliterated, and many inferior elections were made."

Such is the account given by Mr. M. Pattison, whose name in this matter must carry considerable weight, he having been an undergraduate at Oriel during the years 1832 to 1836.

His version of the declension of the college is curiously confirmed by Mr. Thos. Hughes, who speaking of the state of affairs about 1840, the year in which the late Bishop of Manchester was elected to a fellowship, expresses himself thus :—" Be the reason what it may, the battle which was raging in the Church and University round Tract XC., interested Provost and Fellows far more deeply than the ordinary routine work of the college, and that work suffered accordingly. The old tradition, which had obtained even amongst the undergraduates of Oriel who were content with the pass schools—that the cultivation of the intellect was at least one main object of life at the University—still lingered in the college, but only as a tradition. With the exception of Christ Church, there was at this juncture probably no college in Oxford less addicted to reading for the schools, or, indeed, to intellectual work of any kind."

Mr. Hughes' statements are confirmed by what Mr. P. Maurice, Chaplain of New and All Souls' Colleges, asserts in a pamphlet, entitled, *A Key to the Popery of Oxford*, published in 1838. He observes,—" That this speculative divinity has not had any beneficial influence upon the classical studies of the members of Oriel College, may reasonably be inferred from the few names that have appeared among the successful candidates for high academical honours during the three or four past years, and especially during the last year."

Mr. Hughes goes on to record how in the next few years, between 1840 and 1847, the undergraduates of Oriel seldom rose above fifty in number, and how three-quarters of them were wholly given over to athletics, which they cultivated with great success in all branches. He proceeds to say,—" Upon all the pursuits which thus absorbed the energies of their pupils, Provost, Dean and Tutors looked, not only without sympathy, but with scarcely-veiled dislike. No subscriptions, however small, ever came to boat club or cricket club from any of them; nor was any one of them ever seen on the river bank at the races, or on Cowley Marsh at a cricket match. Leave to dine in the middle of the day during the races was only granted to the racing crew after frequent applications, and at last grudgingly. All the tutors were in orders, and none of them, so far as was known, had ever used their legs except for a mild constitutional, or their arms for anything beyond handling editions of the classics, and the fathers, and writing elegant prose and verse in the dead languages."

We must hasten on, however, to the following year, which witnessed the abrupt termination of the long series of *Tracts*, which had given an importance to Oxford such as she had not known since the time when Charles I. quartered himself, his court, and his staff amid her ancient halls, in the days of the great civil war.

We have seen that Mr. Newman found himself compelled to grapple with the thirty-nine Articles of the Church of England; if he would save the teaching and work of the last seven years, he must show that those Articles contained in a living form the principles of Primitive Christianity. His attempt to solve the difficulty took the form of Tract 90, which appeared in January, 1841, its main thesis being this :—the Articles do not oppose Catholic teaching; they but partially oppose Roman dogma; they for the most part oppose the dominant errors of Rome.

The Protestant party in the English Church had always claimed that the Articles were actually drawn up against popery, and that therefore it was absurd and dishonest to suppose that popery in any shape could take refuge under their wing. Newman exploded this notion by pointing out that the Articles were drawn up before the conclusion of the Council of Trent, which had formulated for the first time several of the most grievous errors of Rome.

He showed also that the Articles were unquestionably elastic, for was not the seventeenth assumed by one school of Protestants to be Lutheran, by another to be Calvinistic?

He indicated moreover that the original object of the Articles had been, not to exclude rigidly every Romanist, but rather to comprehend as many Romanists and Protestants as possible in the National Church. He pointed out that the 35th Article refers to the Books of Homilies as containing a " godly and wholesome doctrine, and necessary for their times ; " and then drew out from the said Homilies a long array of passages teaching doctrines which savoured much more of Rome than of Geneva.

He also indicated that the Articles are not a completely satisfactory compendium of true religious doctrine, being, in regard to many questions of importance, vague and undecided.

All Newman's positions were unquestionably true, though there was certainly force in the Protestant answer that if the authors of the Articles could have foreseen the construction which he put upon them, they would probably have protested strongly against it.

This was the ground upon which the hue and cry, which arose immediately upon the appearance of the tract, was based. The Evangelicals considered that the Articles, where their meaning was doubtful, should be interpreted according to the known opinions of those who framed them. Mr. Newman, on the other hand, and his friends Mr. Keble and Dr. Pusey, who at once endorsed the tract, professed that the Articles, where doubtful, should be interpreted according to the mind of the Catholic Church. At the time of its appearance Tract No. 90 was condemned by most common-sense people; since then, however, the tide of feeling in regard to it has turned.

Mr. Molesworth tells us that " the principle of interpretation advanced in Tract No. 90 was strongly censured by Dr. Blomfield, Bishop of London, who, in the year 1842, delivered a triennial charge of remarkable ability to the clergy of his diocese, in St. Paul's Cathedral. This manifesto condemned the practice recommended in the tract of putting interpretations on the Articles which were not warranted by their plain, grammatical sense, and did not convey the intentions and opinions of those by whom the Articles were framed or imposed."

Mr. Daniel Macmillan, founder of the great publishing firm of that name, wrote on April 30, 1841: " This tract pretends to be a defence of the 'Articles,' but is in reality a series of glosses of the most Jesuitical sort, by which the author tries to make out that a man may be three-fourths a Papist and sign the 'Thirty-nine Articles,' and still remain in the Church of England."

Since then men have been able to review the

controversy dispassionately and calmly; they have read, most of them with profit, Newman's *Apologia*; and, to speak generally, they agree with Mr. J. A. Froude that on the charge of dishonesty Newman stands acquitted, and that Tract 90 broke the back of the Thirty-nine Articles.

In 1841, however, the storm gathered quickly, dark, and heavy; before the publication of the Tract, rumours of its contents had got into the hostile camp in an exaggerated form; and not a moment was lost in proceeding to action. Four of the Oxford Tutors—T. T. Churton, Brazenose; H. B. Wilson, S. John's; J. Griffiths, Wadham; and A. C. Tait, Balliol, afterwards well-known as the Archbishop of Canterbury, united in a protest against it which was published on March 8. On March 10 the Vice-Chancellor laid Tract 90, with the protest of the four Tutors, before the Board of the Heads of Houses. A committee of Heads, to examine the Tract, was named on Friday the 12th. On Saturday Mr. Newman wrote, with marvellous speed, an explanatory pamphlet in the form of a letter to Dr. Jelf, Canon of Christ Church. On Sunday he and others wrote to the Vice-Chancellor requesting that judgment might be withheld till after the publication of the letter to Dr. Jelf, which was already in the press. The Board's condemnation, however, was published on Monday 15, anticipating Mr. Newman's promised explanation by a few hours.

Towards the end of March the Bishop of Oxford wrote to Newman, begging him, for the sake of peace, to suppress the Tract. Newman could not do this, but consented not to publish any more. On April 2 he wrote the Bishop an explanatory letter, which was published in the course of a few days, and to which the Bishop gave his unqualified approbation. The condemnation, however, of the Tract by the Heads of Houses, and the storm of indignation throughout the country, impressed Newman with the conviction, to quote his own words, that " my place in the movement was lost; public confidence was at an end; my occupation was gone. It was simply an impossibility that I could say anything henceforth to good effect, when I had been posted up by the Marshall on the buttery-hatch of every College of my University, after the manner of discommoned pastry-cooks, and when in every part of the country and every class of society, through every organ and opportunity of opinion, in newspapers, in periodicals, at meetings, in pulpits, at dinner tables, in coffee-rooms, in railway carriages, I was denounced as a traitor who had laid his train and was detected in the very act of firing it against the time-honoured establishment."

Having retired from the leadership of the movement, Mr. Newman found himself in the summer of 1841 at Littlemore, without any great difficulty to oppress him. He says: " I had determined to put aside all controversy, and I set myself down to my translation of St. Athanasius; but between July and November, I received three blows that broke me."

1.—" I had got but a little way in my work when my trouble returned to me. The ghost had come a second time. In the Arian history I found the very same phenomenon, in a far bolder shape, which I had found in the Monophysite. I had not observed it in 1832 . . . . I saw clearly that in the history of Arianism the pure Arians were the Protestants, the semi-Arians were the Anglicans, and that Rome now was what it was then. The truth lay, not with the *Via Media*, but with what was called 'the extreme party.'"

2.—" I was in the misery of this new unsettlement when a second blow came upon me. The bishops, one after another, began to charge against me. It was a formal determinate movement."

3.—" As if all this were not enough, there came the affair of the Jerusalem bishopric."

The English and Prussian Governments were at this time uniting to found a new bishopric, as a bulwark for the spiritual interests of Protestants residing at Jerusalem. Newman regarded this act of communion, with heretical German Protestants, as almost destroying the claim of the Church of England to be considered a branch of the true Catholic Church. From this time forward he was, to use his own words, "on my death-bed, as regards my membership with the Anglican Church, though at the time I became aware of it only by degrees." He goes on a few lines later to add—" A death-bed has scarcely a history; it is a tedious decline, with seasons of rallying and seasons of falling back ; and, since the end is foreseen, or what is called a matter of time, it has little interest for the reader, especially if he has a kind heart."

Newman's Anglican death-bed may be described in a few words. One after another the bishops attacked him in their charges, driving home upon his mind the conviction that the highest authorities did not regard his interpretation of the Articles as tenable by an honest English Churchman. Thirlwall, with the acutest intellect and the most judicial mind on the Bench, being the one exception.

Angry guardians, whose wards had gone over to Rome, wrote to Newman asking him to convert them back again. He could only reply sadly that, had not Tract 90 been condemned they would have been Anglicans still.

He endeavoured to live at Littlemore, together with a number of younger disciples, a life of meditation, self-discipline, and prayer, only to be subjected to every species of impertinence. He had to repel even the insolently curious questioning of his bishop, not to speak of the intrusions of less important and less responsible persons. To quote his own words—" I cannot walk into or out of my house but curious eyes are upon me. Why will you not let me die in peace? Wounded brutes creep into some hole to die in, and no one grudges it them ..... One day when I entered my house I found a flight of undergraduates inside. Heads of houses, as mounted patrols, walked their horses round those poor cottages. Doctors of divinity dived into the inner recesses of that private tenement uninvited, and drew domestic conclusions from what they saw there."

On one occasion a prominent and flourishing Oxford Evangelical, expecting to find Newman out, called at his house at Littlemore. To the good man's surprise Newman himself, instead of the maid, opened the door. He could only ask to look over the Monastery. It was a gratification to Newman to be able to say, "There is no monastery here," and then to slam the door in the foolish fellow's face.

In 1833, in consequence of the premature perversion to Rome of one of his disciples at Littlemore, who had promised shortly before to wait at least three years, Newman felt bound in honour to resign S. Mary's, and for the two next years he remained in lay communion with the Church of England.

During the years 1841 to 1845 he was also the pained spectator of many virulent attacks upon the dearest of his friends, who had been most closely associated with him in the work of the movement. In the latter part of 1841, on Mr. Keble's resignation of the University Professorship of Poetry, there ensued a contest which became simply a trial of strength between the High and Low schools of theological opinion. The candidates were Mr. Garbett (Evangelical) and Mr. Isaac Williams, the author of the well-known *Tracts on Reserve*, which had been the objects of so much hostile criticism. Canon Ashwell, in his *Life of Bishop Wilberforce*, states in a footnote—" The committees of the respective candidates agreed to abide by the result of a comparison of the number of promises of support which they had received, when it was found that there were, for Mr. Garbett 921 ; for Mr. Isaac Williams, 623." An actual contest was thus avoided by the withdrawal of Mr. Williams, though of the two candidates he was unquestionably the best qualified for the post.

Again, in the year 1843, Dr. Pusey preached a sermon at Christ Church on the Holy Eucharist, in which he was alleged to have taught the doctrine of Transubstantiation. The case was tried before the Board of Heresy of the University. Dr. Pusey claimed a hearing but his request was denied, and he was condemned to be suspended from preaching before the University for two years. A protest against this sentence was drawn up and signed by many influential persons, of whom Mr. Gladstone was one, but was refused any notice by the Vice-Chancellor.

In the following year there appeared a celebrated book, entitled, *The Ideal of a Christian Church*, by Mr. W. G. Ward, a Fellow of Balliol College, one of the ablest of Mr. Newman's lieutenants, who "had been instantaneously converted to Newman by a single line in an introduction to one of his works, to the effect that Protestantism could never have corrupted into Popery. Ward was a person of great weight in the University, a good all round man, a great musical critic, and an admirable buffo singer. He also had the gift of grasping practical truths and expressing them in terms likely to be remembered.

Mr. T. W. Allies, in *A Life's Dicision*, writes thus :—" I was disgusted with old Howley—especially with his 'moderation' and 'venerableness.' In these words, I was thinking, without applying it, of Ward's remark,—' If a man be called moderate or venerable, beware of him; but if both, you may be sure he is a scoundrel.'"

However, in *The Ideal of a Christian Church*, Mr. Ward took a still more objectionable view of the articles than that which Newman had propounded in Tract 90, besides in other ways avowing undisguised sympathy with Rome. "To sum up the difference in one sentence, Mr. Newman would have drawn out a Catholic sense *from* the Articles; Mr. Ward would have imported a *Roman* Catholic sense into them."

On Feb. 13, 1845, the case was brought before the Convocation of the University, more than 1,200 members having come up from all parts of the kingdom. Mr. Ward made a long speech in explanation of certain passages, which it had been proposed should be condemned. The proposition or vote of condemnation was carried by 777 to 386. Then a proposition for the degradation of Mr. Ward from his degrees was carried, though by a much smaller majority. A third proposition for the condemnation of Tract No. 90 was then submitted to the assembly, but the proctors, Mr. Guillemard and Mr. Church, now Dean of St. Paul's, rose and exercised their ancient right of veto, thus stopping any further proceedings.

During the last years of his life as an Anglican, Newman had many difficulties to contend with besides those arising from the hostility of popular Protestant opinion. He was compromised by the turbulent independence, and his own freedom of thought was hampered by the pertinacious curiosity of the younger disciples of the movement.

Between 1841 and 1845 a certain change took place in the character of the movement which Mr. Newman describes as follows: " A new school of thought was rising, as is usual in doctrinal inquiries, and was sweeping the original party of the movement aside, and was taking its place."

The leading spirits in this younger branch of the brotherhood were Mr. Ward, to whom we have just alluded, and Mr. Oakely. They were "somehow as much associated as Castor and Pollux, Damon and Pythias, or any two unseparable pairs. The points in common between these were that they were both Balliol men, great names in the University, and very considerable personages to come spontaneously from a distant part of the sphere, to a centre of attractions which did not invite everybody. Both of them, having received their new impulses, went ahead, disregarded warnings, and defied control. As it had been entirely their own choice to come, so they consulted their own choice in going on." Such is the account given by Mr. Mozley of this remarkable pair. Dr. Newman tells us how "these men cut into the original movement at an angle, fell across its line of thought, and then set about turning that line in its own direction. They were most of them keenly religious men, with a true concern for their souls as the first matter of all, with a great zeal for me, but giving little certainty at the time as to which way they would ultimately turn. Some in the event have remained firm to Anglicanism, some have become Catholics, and some have found a refuge in Liberalism."

Mr. J. A. Froude was for a time one of this younger school, and was employed by Mr. Newman, along with others, in the year 1843, to write a series of lives of the English saints. The result of an investigation into the authenticity and credibility of mediæval legends, severed Mr. Froude from the Tractarian party.

Dr Hook's biographer, speaking of the events of these years, remarks: "A new party seemed to be rising, as different in its teachings from the original Tractarians as they had been from the Evangelicals: a party pointing to the mediæval rather than the primitive Church as the pattern of all that was excellent in doctrine and practice; viewing the English reformers and their work with suspicion, if not aversion, the Romanists with leniency and favour."

Sober-minded, quiet men like Pusey, Keble, and Isaac Williams were powerless to turn this new tide of feeling into a more healthy channel. Had Hurrell Froude lived, and remained loyal to the Church of England, he might possibly have held the reins, which had now fallen from Newman's hands, for in 1843 the latter turned his face Rome-wards and withdrew, as far as possible during the next two years from influencing others. He says, "My only line, my only duty was to keep simply to my own case. I recollect Pascal's words, '*Je mouvrai seul.*' I deliberately put out of my thoughts all other works and claims, and said nothing to anyone, unless I was obliged."

It was impossible, however, that Newman should then be left alone; there were numbers of persons in all parts of England, who watched for his every word, who wished to follow him whithersoever he went, and who were constantly writing to him, asking him to explain this or that mis-statement in the newspapers, and to tell them what he himself was thinking and purposing, and what they should themselves think and purpose.

He himself wrote in 1841, "I speak most sincerely when I say that there are things which I neither contemplate, nor wish to contemplate; but, when I am asked about them ten times, at length I begin to contemplate them."

Dr. Russell, afterwards the President of the Roman College at Maynooth, had called upon Newman in Oxford in the summer of 1841; and then, or afterwards, placed certain books in his hands, which influenced him considerably in the direction of the step, which he finally took in 1845.

The years, which we are considering, were unquestionably a season of grievous disaster at Oxford, but about the same time the light of the new day was beginning to break upon the sister University of Cambridge. Dean Stanley (we quote from memory) once observed that it "has been the part of Oxford to give birth to great movements, that of Cambridge to send forth great men." However that may be, no great movement has ever yet carried Cambridge off her legs. She sits upon the shore and watches the tide roll by, and then calmly and carefully gathers whatever of value has been thrown up.

The writer of a leader in the *Guardian*, commemo-

rating Mr. Beresford Hope, who took his degree at Cambridge in 1841, speaking of that period observes:—
"The religious revival had stirred Cambridge, but it touched different points from Oxford, and worked in a different way. There is no trace at Cambridge, as far as we know, of the perilous speculations, and the fierce repression that went on at Oxford. Mr. Hope was one of a set of men who welcomed with interest and sympathy the new religious movement, but who accepted it among themselves on its practical side. The questions which sent the Oxford men to Rome certainly did not disturb University life at Cambridge. The Cambridge men, accepting the great idea of the Catholic Church, set themselves to work out how the outward aspects of English public worship might be made most reasonably and intelligently to correspond to the ideals and the best traditions of the ancient and historic Church. They founded the Camden Society, and the *Ecclesiologist*, to carry on this study with characteristic breadth and thoroughness. And they took a great and eventful step; for it was the condition, the indispensable condition, of bringing the ideas which had been worked out at Oxford into touch with the popular mind. The work begun by those Cambridge men has changed the whole face of public worship in England; and in this work Mr. Hope from the first took a leading part." (*The Guardian*, Oct. 26, 1887.)

A writer in the same paper, in an obituary article on the late W. H. Guillemard, who took his B.A. degree in 1838, and was very shortly afterwards elected Fellow of Pembroke College, speaking of his life during the few years which immediately followed, observes—"At this time Cambridge was feeling the first influence of the Oxford movement. Simeon was recently dead. The evangelical tradition had passed into feebler hands. Professor Blunt had been elected Margaret Professor, and was delivering the courses of lectures which did so much to revive the study of patristic theology, and to raise the ideal of the life and work of the parish priest. Dr. Mill had returned from Calcutta and was settled at Cambridge, and was preaching the University morning sermons at St. Mary's to a scanty but highly appreciative congregation. Philip Freeman, the future Archdeacon of Exeter, who had been transplanted from Trinity to the Tutorship of Peterhouse, had startled the decorous, sleepy Church of Englandism of Cambridge by a vigorous pamphlet directed against the neglect of the rules of the Church in the services of the chapels and churches, and in the daily life of the University; while private religious gatherings were encouraged, true Church principles were entirely forgotten, or mentioned only to be denounced as tending to Popery.

"Peterhouse is near Pembroke, and Freeman and Guillemard soon became fast friends and fellow-labourers, in company with a few like-minded men, for the restoration of Anglican faith and practice. About this time the Cambridge Camden Society was established by John Mason Neale, Benjamin Webb and Edward Boyce." (*The Guardian*, September 14, 1887.)

Up to the last, however, friends of Newman's at Oxford, hoped against hope that the English Church might keep him; but at length on October 9, 1845, he wrote as follows to Mr. Allies, a friend who was a few years later to follow him to the same bourne:—"I am to be received into what I believe to be the one Church and the one Communion of Saints this evening, if it is so ordained. Father Dominic, the Passionist, is here, and

I have begun my confession to him. I suppose two friends will be received with me. May I have only one tenth part as much faith as I have intellectual conviction where the truth lies. I do not suppose any one can have had such combined reasons poured upon him that he is doing right. So far I am most blessed; but, alas! my heart is so hard, and I am taking things so much as a matter of course, that I have been quite frightened lest I should not have faith and contrition enough to gain the benefit of the sacrament. Perhaps faith and reason are incompatible in one person, or nearly so."

It is not for any man to say that Father Newman was wrong in taking the final step. God has seen fit to leave to Rome the earthly guidance of the spiritual life of uncounted millions of our race. And who shall say that Newman was not obeying a true *call* from above. It is much easier to lament his decision than to prove satisfactorily that it was wrong. He strove for years to rouse the Church of his own people to a sense of its shortcomings and its dangers. And to quote from *The Nemesis of Faith*, " What was his reward? He was denounced as a Cassandra prophet; bid go, get him gone, shake the dust from off his feet and depart to his own place. He took them at their word, and left the falling house, not without scorn. A little more slumber, a little more sleep. It was the sluggard's cry, let them find the sluggard's doom."

CHAPTER VI.

THE RESULTS.

THE secession of Mr. Newman to the Church of Rome on October 9th, 1845, came to many anxious hearts as a great shock, while to others it seemed to promise, and, in fact, did bring, a welcome calm after long years of controversy, anxiety and doubt. The former were asking themselves whether, Newman having gone, they could honestly themselves remain; whether it might not be well to escape from the falling house; whether, if Roman claims had satisfied the intellect of their great leader, they might not surely themselves find peace under the shadow of her all-sheltering wing. They might have found the last question more difficult of decision could they have listened to the words of the Sovereign Pontiff, then seated in the chair of S. Peter, who, to a tearfully despondent lady, asking if he did not fear for the Bark of Peter, replied that "he was under no apprehension on account of the Bark, but he felt some doubts as to what might be the fate of the crew."

A letter, written on October 19 to his mother, by James Fraser, then Fellow of Oriel, afterwards the Man of Manchester, is both characteristic of the writer and also interesting as showing the light in which Newman's secession was regarded: "When a man of Newman's surpassing intellect, and unquestioned holiness, self-denial and piety—in which respects I haver yet seen any man worthy to be put in comparison with him (except, perhaps, Dr. Pusey)—when a man whose very

presence, even his silent presence, casts a mysterious influence for good on all around him, feels what he deems an imperative call to leave that Church in which he was baptised, and of which he has been a minister, I think that those who feel most satisfied and confident of their own position may well suspect that there are some serious deficiencies in a system in which the aspirations of such a spirit as his could meet with no corresponding voice, and find no sympathetic aid." . . . .
" His departure from among us is much felt, even by those who differed from his views, where his urbanity and manners, no less than his exalted intellect and eminent piety, had much endeared him. There may be a few who are foolish or shortsighted, or malicious enough to rejoice at it, but I am happy to say they are but few. The general feeling is one of deep regret, not unaccompanied by anxious queries, ' What is to become of the Church of England?' But I have taken up too much of your time with this painful subject, which the business of the last week has brought so vividly to our minds. To change the subject. Has Jones found me out some hay and straw yet? Remember the price of the former was not to exceed £4 10s., nor the latter £2 10s. a ton."

A striking picture of the state of the case! Newman was gone in search of pastures new; but the secular cares of those whom he had left, down to the provision for the wants of the brute creation, still remained. There is no record of even the slightest fall of English Stocks in consequence of the loss which the National Church had just sustained. Writers of a certain theological school, and with a certain sense or non-sense of practical perspective, assure us *ore rotundo* that at this great crisis in the history of the movement the future of the Church of England rested in the hands of Dr. Pusey!!

As a matter of fact, had Pusey followed Newman it is possible that a few score more of the clergy might have followed the two great leaders—(whether Rome would have welcomed them all is another matter)—but the effect upon the great body of the laity would have been inappreciable.

During the few years which followed Newman's departure there was a slight, and somewhat intermittent, trickle of perverts, among whom the most distinguished were perhaps Archdeacon Manning, Archdeacon Wilberforce, Mr. Ward, Mr. Oakeley, Mr. Faber, Mr. Allies, and Miss Giberne. The most noteworthy of the secessionists were persons who thought it better *errare cum Platone*, than to go to heaven with Archbishop Howley, and their attitude towards the great question is, perhaps, fitly described in a note of Mr. Allies, dated Nov. 5, 1845, in which after describing a recent visit to Newman at Littlemore, subsequent to his perversion, he adds—" It was a great delight to see him again. One just feels that one would be content to do anything and to go anywhere with him."

And what, it may be asked, has been Dr. Newman's reward? Rome could not afford to allow so great a prize to slip out of her net, but it has been generally understood that his well-known obedience to conscience, and the keenness of his intellect, for many years prevented the highest authorities of the Church of his adoption, from trusting or rewarding him according to his deserts.

A writer in *The World* has pointed out how " No two sets of ideas could be more dissimilar than those respectively suggested by the man John Henry Newman, and the place Birmingham. And yet in Birmingham is Dr. Newman's home. There the late Cardinal Wiseman placed him in 1848, and there he still remains. An ugly red-brick building, shaped in the most modern of modern styles, in a suburb full of other ugly red-brick buildings, with a narrow strip of ground before it planted with dingy shrubs, standing back a little from the street, as if overshadowed by the grandeur of the neighbouring bank and inn—such is the place where Dr. Newman's dwelling is fixed."

For this he left the beauty, the mellowed antiquity, and the intellectual converse of Oxford, ever so dear to him. The well-remembered spires, the domes and towers, he did not see again, except as a passing traveller from the railway, for thirty-two years after he left there at the bidding of conscience on February 23, 1846.

At Birmingham he was placed and, with the exception of the seven years he spent in Dublin—essaying, at the bidding of authority, the conduct of a great college, under impossible conditions—there he has since remained —" in port, as he has told us, after a rough sea ; willingly taking, as he elsewhere says, that humble place of service which his superiors chose for him, the desire of his heart and his duty going together ; determined not to have the praise or the popularity which the world can give, but, according to St. Philip Neri's precept, to love to be unknown."

It is notorious, however, how in 1864 he was forced from his obscurity by a well-intentioned, but quite unjustifiable attack, on the part of Mr. Kingsley, who accused him by name of teaching that truth for its own sake was not, and, on the whole, ought not to be, a virtue with the Roman clergy. This attack was answered by the publication of Dr. Newman's *Apologia pro Vitâ Suâ*, in which the veil was lifted from the first forty-five years of his inner life, and there were traced all the windings of the road, by which he had travelled from the Calvinism of his childhood to the faith of the Vatican. It was "a narrative whose simple candour carried conviction even to theological opponents. Few books have so triumphantly accomplished their purpose as that remarkable work. It is not too much to say that a revolution in the popular estimate of the author was caused by it."

Dr. Newman, in his later years, like Lacordaire, the great teacher of the Church of France, has returned from the instruction of men to the training of youth, and for many years his chief interest has been that of the "Oratory School, his own creation, in which, under his fostering care, the youths of some of the greatest Catholic families are trained in traditions of scholarship and conduct transplanted from the old national seats of education, but modified or transformed by his judgment, and impressed, if we may so speak, with his personality." In a parlour of his house hangs a print of Oxford, with the inscription underneath, "Fili hominis putas ne vivent ossa ista? Et dixi, Domine Deus, tu nosti."

The tranquil course of Dr. Newman's life has been "broken at rare intervals by visits to old and cherished friends, chiefly of his Oxford days, or by retirement to a tiny country house of the Oratorians, a few miles distant at Rednall, round which is the little churchyard where they are buried."

For many years after the crisis of 1845, Dr. Pusey and Mr. Keble survived, the unquestioned chiefs of the party of the Movement: the former as acting commandant at headquarters, the latter at Hursley as the general referee, without whose counsel no question of importance was decided. A commissioner of *The World* reported in 1878:—" At Oxford, in Christ Church, in the canonical residence which he has occupied for nearly half-a-century, Dr. Pusey still remains. There he has lived, laboured, taught; and there he will live to the end. It is a home which has been in its time the scene of many pilgrimages, of many visits of a widely different order— college dignitaries and tutors coming on purely official business; bishops and statesmen, former college intimates, coming partly for personal, partly for public, reasons; 'Students of the House' desirous to discuss points of University discipline; country clergymen from all parts of England; undergraduates of many successive generations, who have wished to consult Dr. Pusey on spiritual matters, and whose confidence Dr. Pusey himself may have considered it desirable to gain." ... "There is an absence of all those signs of luxurious æstheticism which are so conspicuous a feature in the modern collegiate life at Oxford, as well as in the domestic establishments which in their latter days have grown up under the shadow of the cloister. There are no miniature conservatories in the windows, no gaily striped curtains, no crimson blinds. The hall-door is opened by no smart butler or trim waiting maid; the foot falls upon no rich yielding Axminster or Brussels carpet. Everything is plain, simple, severe. The janitress is a middle-aged woman in a plain print dress; the only covering which the floor of the hall and the passage knows is a thin strip of cocoa-nut matting. The whole air of the place is rather that of a country vicarage, whose vicar is in reduced circumstances, or of an academic residence before the innovating influences of metropolitan refinement and pomp had made their way to the Isis." The same intelligent writer goes on to describe the tenant of the dwelling. " There is nothing in the exterior or in the raiment of the short, stoutish little gentleman, who rises to greet you, to say certainly that he is a clergyman, still less to remind you that he is the great assertor of the spiritual independence of the Church. The chief visible suggestion of his sacred calling is the surplice thrown on a couch, and that in Oxford is a not unusual feature even in the layman's room. From head to foot Dr. Pusey, indeed, is clad in black; but then black is also affected by many gentlemen of the old school who are not divines, and Dr. Pusey might well be, from his appearance, such another tory squire as his friend and senior, Mr. J. W. Henley. The coat is buttoned close up to the neck, with a very narrow interspace of white visible; the massive and powerful head, with its copious growth of grey hair, is surmounted with a skull-cap of black silk, of somewhat loose and ill-constructed fit. But the two most remarkable features about Dr. Pusey are his eyes and mouth. The latter is mobile with every kind of expression; the former are a deep blue, perfectly clear, free from the aqueous film of age, varying as the mouth does, with the thought which animates the mind or proceeds in language from the lips. Never could there be a more speaking face, never a face in which there was concentrated more of the blended sentiments or capacities, of earnestness, humour, solemn intensity, subtle satire. It is impossible not to be impressed by the perfect breeding, the true patrician ease, the masterly *savoir-faire*, which make up Dr. Pusey's manner." There for more than half a century, Dr. Pusey, his chief characteristic being stationariness, spent a long life of unremitting toil—writing, lecturing, preaching, directing, hearing confessions, until some five years ago he was called hence.

Mr. Keble remained at Hursley, a saint in a quiet sort of way, helpful and instructive doubtless to many, a rare example of the devotion of high intellectual gifts to the efficient discharge of the lowliest duties of a country clergyman. A certain deduction from the usefulness of his life was caused by the over-estimate formed of him by some of the more eminent of his party—Keble was a very good, but hardly a great man. Life did not bring him those heaviest troubles, which, if met aright, alone prepare men to exercise the deepest influence on their fellow-creatures. He never knew what it was to want a sovereign, or to stand alone face to face with a number of bitter, determined foes.

Persons, therefore, who pilgrimed to Hursley to take stock of the man, who was reputed to be the great saint of the Anglican Communion, sometimes suffered a slight shock of disappointment. As an example, Mr. Allies, in later years a pervert to Rome, at great cost to himself, speaking of the events of 1845, observes—"Marriott took me to Keble's house at Hursley, which I visited with great interest. The impression which the single day there spent has ever since left on me is that his life was pre-eminently domestic—with a wife and a sister to his heart he shut himself out from the roaring of the blast which pierced me through and through. That is, his life exemplified his words—

> Nor strive to wind ourselves too high
> For sinful man beneath the sky."

Confessor or martyr he was not made to be, but an ecclesiastical Walton, fishing by the side of quiet streams, and enjoying the lights and shadows as he dangled his trout at the end of his rod: no Athanasius, as I had dreamed, but an Anglican parson."

The charge, too, of inability to prevent disciples from following out the principles of some of the *Tracts* to the bitter end, was brought againt Keble as against other leaders of the movement. Mr. Pattison recording the religious course of a highly-gifted lady, a near relative of his own, observes:—" Her mother, a good and sensible woman, became alarmed, and thought to stop the mischief by removing from Yorkshire to some place where Anglican privileges could be enjoyed in their plenitude. No place could surely surpass Hursley in this respect; and to Hursley they went. But it was too late. The daughter had got the Roman fever in her veins; everything about the services at Hursley was contemptible, disgusting, odious, and Keble himself, so far from being a saint, was discovered to be an addle-headed old hypocrite. Of course, there was nothing for it after this; my cousin was received into the Church of Rome, and compelled her mother, who lived but for her daughter, to go in with her." .... " All intellectual intercourse between myself and my cousin was at an end. Her conversation had come to be a passionate invective in monologue against Protestantism, Anglicanism, and everything except what was Roman. They lived about a great deal in Italy, etc., afterwards, and had every opportunity of seeing the seamy side of practical Catholicism; but my cousin saw it not. .... Can such a wreck of a noble intellect by religious fanaticism be paralleled." But to return to one of the statements with which we begun this chapter, to the effect that to some Newman's secession seemed to bring calm after a long continuance of broken weather.

Mr. Pattison narrates how—" It is impossible to describe the enormous effect produced in the academical and clerical world, I may say throughout England, by one man's changing his religion. But it was not consternation; it was a lull—a sense that the past agitation of twelve years was extinguished by this simple act; and perhaps a lull of expectation to see how many he would take with him. Instead of a ferocious howl, Newman's proceeding was received in respectful silence, no one blaming." ....

"The truth is that this moment, which swept the leader of the Tractarians, with most of his followers, out of the place, was an epoch in the history of the University. It was a deliverance from the nightmare which had oppressed Oxford for fifteen years. For so long we had been given over to discussions, unprofitable in themselves, and which had entirely diverted our thoughts from the true business of the place. Probably there was no period of our history during which, I do not say science and learning, but the ordinary study of the classics was so profitless or at so low an ebb as during the period of the Tractarian Controversy. By the secessions of 1845 this was extinguished in a moment, and from that moment dates the regeneration of the University. Our thoughts reverted to their proper channel—that of the work we had to do."

To the same effect Mr. J. A. Froude, after speaking of the ignorance, the neglect of study, the wastefulness which prevailed among the undergradutes during the years of the *Tracts*, goes on to observe—"In all this there was room and to spare for reforming energy, and it may be said that the administration of the University was the immediate business of the leading members—a business, indeed a duty, much more immediate than the unprotestantizing of the Church of England. But there was no leisure—there was not even a visible desire to meddle with concerns so vulgar. Famous as the Tractarian leaders were to become, their names are not connected with a single effort to improve the teaching at Oxford, or to mend its manners. Behind the larger conflict which they raised, that duty was left untouched for many years; it was taken up ultimately by the despised Liberals, who have not done it well, but have at least accomplished something, and have won the credit which was left imprudently within their reach."

To these practical results in Oxford, the home of the movement, we have directed the reader's attention, believing them to have not yet received that amount of popular recognition which was their due.

To other results, which do not affect Oxford so much as the Church of England in general, and which have therefore been widely acknowledged and insisted on, we shall now, in conclusion, briefly advert.

Unquestionably a great deal has to be scored on the credit side of the account, though a certain amount of discount—in some cases a heavy percentage—has to be deducted from most of the items. The friends of the movement tell us that it has greatly raised the personal and ministerial character of the English clergy as a body.

Certainly it has, in the sense that it is not usual for the clergy to take too much to drink on Saturday nights, though it must be added that many of the High Church Clergy have been among the most bitter opponents of the Total Abstinence movement, leaving its defence to the Romanists, the Evangelicals, and the Dissenters.

The present writer, however, feels bound to state, that he learnt the principle of Total Abstinence fifteen years ago from the present Vicar of All Saints, Margaret Street.

To their great credit, the Ritualists, the children of the Tractarians, have striven valiantly, shoulder to shoulder, with a few Evangelicals and Broad Churchmen, for the free and open, and unappropriated system of seating in our Churches.

It is said that the whole method of parish work has been revolutionised by the movement. The statement is no doubt true in regard to town parishes, but in scattered rural districts, earnest clergy now have to do their work on much the same lines as earnest men did fifty years ago.

And, in regard to the town parishes, the new state of things, while it has its advantages, is also qualified by certain drawbacks. Organisations of all kinds have largely increased; the object being the laudable one, of meeting the wants or the tastes of various classes of persons in the most acceptable ways.

Still there is something to be said for the plan of doing one thing well, rather than half-a-dozen things indifferently. And we venture to think that a man had better give one address after six hours' preparation, than six addresses with one hour's preparation for each.

It is also more cheerful, as well as more useful, to get fifty people to a meeting of any kind, than ten or twelve people to each of five meetings.

The over-multiplicity of arrangements is telling moreover prejudicially on the clerical profession.

The increase in the number of assistant curates has been in excess of the increase of independent benefices. Consequently there is a larger number than ever before of clergy waiting for preferment. Certainly the curates of to-day are better paid than those of sixty years ago, but it is greatly to be feared that English gentlemen will not deem it a right or desirable thing to educate and influence their sons in the direction of Holy Orders, knowing that very probably on reaching middle life they may find themselves without any independent sphere of work, liable to be dismissed at any time by a rector—who may himself have obtained preferment by means to which a man of really high character would have been unable to condescend—their value in the market depreciating year by year, thankfully accepting in sheer desperation at five-and-forty, after more than twenty years' hard work, a retired country parish worth two hundred a year.

Again, the spread of the Movement has tended to draw a large number of the most promising young men round certain centres, to the neglect of the more remote and less attractive stations. It seems almost incredible that Bishops should have seen their way to license, and vicars to engage, as many as eight, ten, or twelve curates to serve at the same time in such parishes as those of S. Mary Abbot, Kensington; S. Peter's, Eaton Square; or the Parish Church, at Leeds; while there have been poor, unattractive spheres, within a mile or two, where hard-working vicars are scarcely able to get assistants at all, either for love or money.

It is only natural that young men should like the *éclat* of being attached to spheres of work distinguished by great reputations; and the system certainly pays the rectors and vicars of the said spheres, for they usually become Bishops, or at least Deans; whether the arrangement is right is, however, quite another matter.

Once more, it is said that the Catholic revival has

transformed the appearance of our churches, and the character of our services. Certainly it has been one of the prime factors in producing the change, but it must be remembered that the gradual advance in the popular knowledge of music, and in the general perception of brightness, smartness, and outward decency has greatly helped the Church on its way in this direction.

We are reminded that the Movement has stamped upon people's minds the fact that they may naturally open their griefs, and confess their sins, to the priest of God's Church and receive absolution, or ghostly counsel and advice.

Granted that it be so. Granted, as it should be, that the undergraduates in our great seats of learning, and our medical students, have an important advantage over their grandfathers in knowing that they can without difficulty find priests, who will not be surprised to hear how they have snatched the fruit of the knowledge of good and evil, and who may lead them to the foot of the Tree of Life. Granted, too, as it must be, that many a soul has found in the voluntary self-abasement of confession (without any opinion one way or the other about the validity of priestly absolution) a peace which nothing in this world had ever given them before.

Granted all this, still the broad fact remains—that the enormous majority of Anglican penitents during the past fifty years have been foolish girls, who may probably, in the aggregate, have got as much harm from it as good.

We are pointed to the religious communities of women as one of the best fruits of the Movement. We are unable —we have no wish to deny it. They have achieved results beyond the scope of any other form of Christian endeavour. The course of the work remains unbroken, for though the members pass away the society remains. But, human nature being what it is, even sisterhoods *cannot* be the ideal earthly heavens which some enthusiastic persons imagine them.

www.ingramcontent.com/pod-product-compliance
Lightning Source LLC
Chambersburg PA
CBHW020249170426
43202CB00008B/294